GET
BACKED
GET BIG GET
BOUGHT

GET Colin Barrow
BACKED
GET BIG GET
BOUGHT

Plan your start-up
with the end in mind

CAPSTONE

This edition first published 2009
© 2009 Colin Barrow

Registered office
Capstone Publishing Ltd. (A Wiley Company), The Atrium, Southern Gate, Chichester, West Sussex, PO19 8SQ, United Kingdom

For details of our global editorial offices, for customer services and for information about how to apply for permission to reuse the copyright material in this book please see our website at www.wiley.com.

Library of Congress Cataloging-in-Publication Data

Barrow, Colin.
   Get backed, get big, get bought : plan your start-up with the end in mind / Colin Barrow.
       p. cm.
   Includes index.
   ISBN 978-1-906465-51-3 (pbk.)
   1. Business planning.   2. New business enterprises.
3. Entrepreneurship.   4. Success in business.   I. Title.
   HD30.28.B36852 2006
   658.1'1–dc22

                                                        2009009706

A catalogue record for this book is available from the British Library.

Set in 11 on 12.5 pt Adobe Garamond by SNP Best-set Typesetter Ltd., Hong Kong
Printed in UK by TJ International

Contents

Introduction: Be careful what you wish for

Every year, millions of people start their own business. They come from every walk of life and social group. As many over-50s as under-25s launch out on their own. The same is true for women and men, immigrants and natives, the educated and the barely literate, the brave and the timid, those with creative genius or the self-confessed plodders. The triggers that unleash their desire to go into business are equally eclectic. Legacy, redundancy, boredom and relocation vie with insight and inspiration in the lexicon of sources of their business ideas.

They do, however, all have one common thread, one that is often unspoken but none the less present. They hope they will 'make it'. By that they usually mean make it rich, become super successful and build a business empire. They rarely mention this ambition to the armies of researchers who are continuously trying to unravel entrepreneurial motivators. All these people hear are phrases such as 'personal satisfaction', 'for fun', 'being able to do my own thing', 'working without having to rely on others', 'reducing stress and anxiety', and 'creating employment'. All worthy goals no doubt, but they could all be achieved a whole lot more easily with a few million in the bank.

True, North Americans and many Asians are less ambivalent about being upfront about their desire to be successful in business and make a pile of dough, but there is still a certain nervousness about admitting to having serious wealth creation as a primary goal.

But here's the thing. The majority of businesses start small and stay small. There's nothing much wrong with that, although if that's the limit of your ambition, this book is not for you. This book is for people who want the chance to be seriously rich rather than just seriously busy.

AIM HIGH

Unsurprisingly, only a few tens of thousands of the millions who start up in business each year will become millionaires. And the rest? Well, many of these businesses will indeed make a living for their founder, sometimes even a comfortable one, and they may even be fun to run. But one thing you can reasonably sure about – these founders won't get rich. Instead, they will be embarking on a regime of long hours, sleepless nights and short holidays, and for a significant minority, the bankruptcy courts.

It doesn't have to be this way, but unfortunately most business founders start out with the wrong goals, and so begin businesses that don't have even the potential to make them rich. Aim low and you are almost certain to end up there. Starting a business with the potential to be extremely valuable can take no more overall effort than starting an also-ran. It just requires a different kind of effort and a strategy that will enable you to find investment, grow and ultimately sell up for a big payout.

This is the way of the successful entrepreneur. In a nutshell, the name of the game is get backed, get big and get bought – and that's what this book is all about.

GET
BACKED

Chapter 1

Problems over passion – the real characteristics of winning business ideas

What are the fundamental differences between the great business that will make you seriously rich and the also-ran that does little more than tick over?

That's an important question. A successful business that grows rapidly and establishes a sustainable position in the market will secure your future when the time comes to sell. An under-performing business, on the other hand, will mean long hours of work, often for very little reward. And the truth is that launching a new venture will require a huge amount of energy, commitment and time on your part, so before you fire the starting gun, it's vital to think long and hard about whether your idea has what it takes to deliver the outcome you're seeking.

It's a question that other people will be asking too. Unless you already have considerable personal wealth, at some stage you are going to need to raise the capital that will enable your business idea to blossom and grow. That money might come from wealthy private investors – called business angels – venture capitalists or even family members. All will want to know that your idea has the potential to thrive and provide them with a good return on their cash.

So what should you and your backers be looking for as you assess your business plan? Well, while there are no guarantees in the business world, there are certainly factors that make success more likely. Almost anyone can start a business with great wealth-generating prospects if they plan from the outset to do just that.

But here's the caveat – you have to start with the right formula. There is no mystery to running a successful business. It's been done countless times before and the script has been well and truly written. Put simply, businesses owners who bring together the right ingredients have a fighting chance of creating real wealth. Those who miss out on vital ingredients are almost inevitably doomed to struggle.

The purpose of this book is to map out a journey that will see you creating an business that can be scaled up and ultimately sold. Our first step on that journey is to look at the fundamentals of success. Or to put it another way, we'll be examining the crucial formula that every ambitious business owner should adhere to.

WHAT MAKES AN ENTREPRENEUR?

The first thing that has to be said is that you don't need to be a genius to apply this formula. Entrepreneurs tend to share particular personality traits – a certain quirkiness in the way you think is helpful, as is the ability to put yourself in someone else's shoes – but super intelligence is not essential. Indeed, it has been proven that you don't necessarily need a great education to be a whiz at business. It's a well-known fact that many successful entrepreneurs didn't go to university, or even spend that much time at school. Sir Richard Branson (Virgin) dropped out of full-time education at 16. Sir Alan Sugar (Amstrad), Sir Philip Green (BHS and Arcadia, the group that includes Topshop and Miss Selfridge), Sir Bernie Ecclestone (Formula One – and Britain's tenth richest man) and Charles Dunstone (Carphone Warehouse) all bypassed university education. Many entrepreneurs who went to university didn't stay. Steve Jobs (Apple) and Bill Gates (Microsoft) left after a semester or two; Bruce D. Henderson, founder of world-class management consulting firm the Boston Consulting Group, left Harvard Business School 90 days before graduation, so eager was he to get to work.

Even if your business idea is based on technology or specific knowledge, you can bypass all of the detail, cut to the chase and still make your pile, as the Money Supermarket story shows.

MoneySupermarket.com – a high-tech company with a tried-and-tested business plan

Founded in a bedroom by university opt-outs Simon Nixon and Duncan Cameron in 1999, Money Supermarket grew to have revenues in excess of £100 million barely a decade later. Nixon bailed out of an accounting course at Nottingham University halfway through the second year. He initially worked as a self-employed financial consultant and pursuaded Cameron, a computer geek and his girlfriend's brother, to give up a computer studies course at Liverpool University to write the software programs that were crucial to the launch of the venture.

By the summer of 2007 on the eve of its stock market float Money Supermarket was valued at £1 billion, more than 30 times its previous year's profits. As the name would suggest, the business is an

> Internet-based price comparator that started out in the financial services sector and now covers a myriad of other sectors including utilities, travel and general shopping. The value proposition is that Money Supermarket saves you hours surfing the net yourself. But despite some fairly complicated technology, the business model is little more than the tried-and-tested role of the intermediary or broker doing the sums for their client that Nixon started out with when he began his first business, Mortgage 2000.

On the other hand, you shouldn't worry too much if you do happen to have a university degree. Education is no bar to success in entrepreneurship. Stelios Haji-Iannou, founder of easyJet, graduated from London School of Economics with a BSc in Economics in 1987, following that up with an MSc in Shipping, Trade and Finance from Cass Business School at City University, London. He also has four honorary doctorates from Liverpool John Moores University, Cass Business School, Newcastle Business School and Cranfield University. Tony Wheeler, who together with his wife Maureen founded Lonely Planet Publishing, has degrees from Warwick University and the London Business School. Jeff Bezos (Amazon) is an alumnus of Princeton, Pierre Omidyar (eBay) of Tufts and Google's founders, Sergey Brin and Larry Page, graduated from Stanford.

THE BUILDING BLOCKS OF SUCCESS

So if there is no one template for a successful entrepreneur, what about the business itself? What are the essential building blocks of a world-beating venture?

Some people will tell you that it is helpful to be first into a market with an innovative product or service. Gaining 'first-mover advantage' is often suggested as a proven formula to justify high expenditure and a headlong rush into new markets, the theory being that if you're first in, you can clean up before your competitors get a look in.

This concept is one of the most enduring in business theory and practice. Entrepreneurs and established giants are always in a race to be first. Research from the 1980s claiming to show that market pioneers have enduring advantages in distribution, product-line breadth, product quality and, especially, market share underscores this principle.

Beguiling though the theory of first-mover advantage is, it is almost invariably a mistake to be first. As Gerard Tellis, of the University of Southern California, and Peter Golder, of New York University's Stern Business School, argue in their book *Will and Vision: How Latecomers Grow to Dominate Markets*, it's often those who arrive late to a market who reap the biggest benefits. Early research studies on this subject were based on surveys of surviving companies and brands, excluding all the pioneers that failed. This helps some companies to look as though they were first to market even when they were not. Procter & Gamble (P&G) boasts that it created America's disposable-nappy (diaper) business. In fact, a company called Chux launched its product a quarter of a century before P&G entered the market in 1961.

Also, the questions used to gather much of the data in earlier research were at best ambiguous, and perhaps dangerously so. For example, the term 'one of the pioneers in first developing such products or services' was used as a proxy for 'first to market'. Tellis and Golder emphasise their point by listing popular misconceptions of who were the real pioneers across the 66 markets they analysed. Copiers: Xerox (wrong), IBM (right); PCs: IBM/Apple (both wrong), since Micro Instrumentation Telemetry Systems (MITS) introduced a $400 PC, the Altair, in 1974, followed by Tandy Corporation (Radio Shack) in

11

1977. Nor is the Internet world immune from the benefits of being later to market: Books.com was first into online book sales, but latecomer Amazon was the clear winner.

In fact, the most compelling evidence from all the research is that nearly half of all firms pursuing a first-to-market strategy are fated to fail, while those following fairly close behind are three times as likely to succeed. Tellis and Golder claim that the best strategy is to enter the market after the pioneers, learn from their mistakes, benefit from their product and market development and be more certain about customer preferences.

THE MAGIC FORMULA

So if being first to market is to say the least underrated, what is the magic recipe? Well, you may be surprised to hear that there is one, and that the formula for creating and harvesting a valuable business is not very complicated:

$$V = P \times S \times M \times BE$$

where V = Value, P = Problem, S = Scaleability, M = Money and BE = Barrier to Entry.

Think of it this way. Businesses solve problems for their customers. The bigger the problem, the easier it is to replicate solutions; and the more finance applied, the greater the potential to generate value. A glance at the formula shows why most new ventures are intrinsically valueless. Business starters tend to launch businesses that need few resources, £35,000 is the average start-up investment; rely entirely on the founder, over half of all businesses employ no one other than the founder, a proportion that rises to 80 per cent if employees are capped at 9; and are concentrated on what the business's starter enjoys doing or 'feels a passion for' rather than on solving market problems. If those entrepreneurs wanted to be rich they certainly never listed it as a reason for going into business or gave that subject any thought when choosing which type of business to start or how to go about starting it.

Let's break down each of the components of the magic formula and look at them more closely. We will use a single case example, Tim Waterstone and his eponymous bookstore. This is a neat low-technology venture that has netted Waterstone both a fortune and a place in business history as someone who has changed the way an entire sector works, very much for the better. The book business itself is a useful illustration of the way a product and its distribution systems endure in principle while changing in method over the centuries. From 1403 when the earliest known book was printed from movable type in Korea through to Gutenberg's 42-line Bible printed in 1450, which in turn laid the foundation for the mass book market, the product, at least from a reader's perspective, has changed very little. Even the latest developments of in-store print-on-demand and e-book delivery such as Amazon's Kindle look like leaving the reader holding much the same product.

IDENTIFYING A PROBLEM

Whatever business you are in, look out for problems of sufficient stature to constitute a big P.

When Tim Waterstone was fired from WH Smith's US operation, he was already half way to rethinking the way in which books were to be sold. In the UK the business model comprised rows of books stacked on shelves, spine out in alphabetical order, sectioned off by subject. Bookshops were drab and operated a leisurely 9 to 5 existence, Monday to Friday and only mornings on Saturdays, staffed by assistants with no real understanding of books. In contrast, Manhattan bookshops around where Waterstone lived were brilliant places: lively and consumer led, with huge stock, accessible and knowledgeable staff and long opening hours. The American model addressed several major problems for customers. In the first place, book buyers are usually in a job; were they not they would use a library. So not being open evenings or weekends effectively constrained customers to a quick visit in their lunch break. The second problem concerned the way people browse for books.

Research showed that nearly two thirds of book purchases were unplanned, in the sense that the customer either had no firm idea of what they were looking for or they simply stumbled across an appealing title while in the shop. With this in mind, books had to be distributed around the store to maximise the opportunities for customers to stumble across an interesting title. While the spine-out bookshelf layout was highly economic in terms of floor space and stockholding, it was both unappealing and a further factor limiting sales prospects. The third problem that Waterstone set out to address was to staff his bookshops with people who could offer advice and information on authors and their books. He set out to create an environment that would appeal to literate young graduates rather than to barely articulate shop assistants.

So all in all, Waterstone had identified a number of issues that in combination were big enough to constitute a big P.

SCALE AND THE NEED FOR FINANCE

Big problems require big solutions and this brings us neatly to the question of finance. Had Waterstone simply wanted to open a bookshop, he could have started straightaway. The equity in his house would have been more than enough to finance the venture. But his bookshop concept called for a fundamental change in the way books were to be sold in the UK, which in turn meant, in his opinion, opening a chain of 100 shops. Despite having a comprehensive business plan he found it impossible to get backing. High-street banks turned him down in droves.

But Waterstone had never run a bookshop and he didn't want to. His talent and experience lay in running a business and as such would have been underutilised at best and wasted at worst in trying to set up a single outlet. In any event, the success or otherwise of a single outlet would not prove his business concept conclusively one way or another.

In many ways Waterstone was following a path trodden nearly half a century earlier by Ray Kroc, a milkshake salesman who had first tried his hand at selling paper cups and even worked as a pianist for a while.

McDonald's – scaling up through duplication

Ray Kroc's business travels led him to brothers Richard and Maurice McDonald, who in 1948 had opened the first McDonald's restaurant in San Bernardino, California. Kroc saw that he could fine-tune their restaurant so that it ran like a factory and produced hot food, fast service and with consistent quality no matter where it was located. This could be achieved by breaking food preparation as a process into steps that could be duplicated in any McDonald's restaurant. Kroc wasn't first in the field. Burger King (known then as InstaBurger King) had just opened in Miami. The difference between Kroc and his rivals was one of scale. He took a world-view that saw his franchisees as business partners to be sought out everywhere and not simply as customers to be sold to. His belief was, 'I had to help the individual operator succeed in every way I could.

His success would ensure my success. But I couldn't do that and, at the same time, treat him as a customer.' Kroc sold his new partners an operating system rather than just a licence to use the McDonalds's name, so building a system with near limitless potential. When Kroc died aged 81 ten months before the chain sold its 50 billionth hamburger, he was worth an estimated $500 million.

WHY MONEY MATTERS

Finance can be the defining difference between creating big value and little or no value. Waterstone knew that without investment he could never hope to get his business off the ground. The trick was to find a way of raising enough money to prove the concept, while leaving the door open to raising more once success was in sight. He wrote a detailed business plan and took it round numerous financial institutions. There was little enthusiasm for backing his plan for 100 shops, but with a mixture of money from a finance company, pledging his house, personal savings and borrowings from his father-in-law, and making use of the government's loan guarantee scheme, he raised enough funds to test his strategy. Within three months the first Waterstone's opened, based on a simple store plan that an art student sketched out for £25.

Why the Internet Bookshop was eclipsed by Amazon

UK entrepreneur Darryl Mattocks, a software engineer and computer enthusiast, entered the online bookselling market in 1994, a year ahead of Amazon, but his approach was profoundly different.

Mattocks went into a bookshop in Oxford and picked up a book he had ordered a few days before. He paid for it, walked a few doors down to the Post Office and dispatched it to the customer who had e-mailed his order the previous week. He was constrained initially to financing the business using credit cards, though later a friend introduced him to James Blackwell, a member of the family behind the Oxford booksellers, who put up £50,000 for a 50 per cent stake in the venture.

In contrast, Jeff Bezos, a former investment banker, raised $11 million from Silicon Valley venture capitalists before starting Amazon, and invested $8 million of that in marketing.

Mattocks Internet Bookshop had a database of 16,000 books, while Amazon was selling nearly $16 million worth of books at startup. In 1988, just around the time it was buying Waterstone's, WH Smith bought out bookshop.co.uk, parent company of the Internet Bookshop, for £9.4 million. Amazon was then valued at $10.1 billion.

KEEPING THE COMPETITION AT BAY – BARRIERS TO ENTRY

Once you've found a solution to an important problem and developed a scalable business model to solve that problem, one thing you don't want is to leave the door wide open for others to follow your lead. Sure, they will get there eventually, but it helps if you can recoup some of your investment, catch your second wind and be ready to move on to new, improved versions before they get on your tail. Luckily, the utopian world of perfect competition in which there are many suppliers of identical products or services, with equal access to all the necessary resources such as money, materials, technology and people, doesn't exist except in economics textbooks. You simply need to have a product or service with sufficient unique advantage to make it stand out from others in the market and a barrier to entry preventing others from following the same path to riches. The advantage can be anything – the business name (The Body Shop), a catchy slogan ('Never knowingly undersold', John Lewis), a patented innovation (Dolby Noise Reduction), an instantly recognisable logo (Google) or something similar to Apple's attempts to keep a tight grip on iTunes and the related technology.

Barriers to entry don't have to be high tech or high cost. Midnight hours, Sunday trading (where possible) and bonus schemes for staff were the barriers that Waterstone raised to prohibit the current market leader, WH Smith, from competing head on with his new strategy. Smith's unionised workforce built around retail outlets with a diverse product range made it all but impossible for that company to tread the same path. Waterstone achieved scale quickly, as opening new branches was a well-planned and simple procedure. A handful of head office staff found new locations, bought stock and hired shop managers. Soon the company was employing 500 people in 40 branches, with a turnover of £35 million a year. The ultimate achievement was to sell back the company to WH Smith for £50 million barely a decade after starting up.

COST VERSUS PRICE

One strategy that many would-be new business starters use as their differentiator is low price. The misconception that new firms can undercut established competitors is usually based on ignorance of the true costs of a product or service, a misunderstanding of the meaning and characteristics of overheads and a failure to appreciate that 'unit' costs fall in proportion to experience. This last point is easy to appreciate if you compare the time needed to perform a task for the first time with that required when you are much more experienced (e.g. changing a fuse, replacing a Hoover bag).

The overheads argument usually runs like this: 'They (the competition) are big, have a plush office in Mayfair and lots of overpaid marketing executives, spending the company's money on expense account lunches, and I don't. *Ergo* I must be able to undercut them.' The errors with this type of argument are, first, that the Mayfair office, far from being an 'overhead' in the derogatory sense of the word, may over time be an appreciating asset, perhaps even generating more profit than the company's main products (department stores, restaurants and hotels typically fit into this category); and second, the marketing executives may be paid more than the entrepreneur, but if they don't deliver a constant stream of profit growth they'll be replaced with people who can.

Cost leadership arises through factors such as operating efficiencies and product or service redesign. Ryanair and easyJet are examples where analysing every component of the business made it possible to strip out major elements of cost – meals, free baggage and allocated seating, for example – while leaving the essential proposition – we will fly you from A to B – intact. You don't have to pass on any of the money saved by having cost leadership. Clearly, however, you do have to take account of what your competitors charge, so being unreasonably high will limit your growth prospects. But remember, price is the easiest element of the marketing mix for an established company to vary. It could follow you down the price curve, forcing you into bankruptcy, far more easily than you could capture its customers with a lower price.

A GOOD BEGINNING – GETTING IT RIGHT FROM THE START

Variously listed as a Russian, Vietnamese, Turkish and English proverb, the sentiment 'a good beginning is half the battle' has a powerful resonance in any language. The corollary, 'to get off on the wrong foot', also seems to hold good under a wide range of circumstances. That's exactly what seems to happen when many people start their first business and that's what the magic formula $V = P \times S \times M \times BE$ sets out to prevent.

Let's be absolutely clear. The magic formula is not intended to produce a result such as Douglas Adams' numeric answer to the ultimate question on the meaning of life, the universe and everything, as posed in *The Hitchhiker's Guide to the Galaxy*. In Adams' story, Deep Thought, a computer built specifically for this purpose, takes 7.5 million years to compute and check the answer, which turns out to be 42.

Applying the magic formula certainly won't require a giant computer, nor will it take anything like 7.5 million years to work through. You may also be slightly disappointed, though hopefully not too much so, to learn that the formula doesn't produce a single numeric answer. In fact, the answer may well not have any numbers in it all. The formula's sole purpose is to make sure you set off on the right track from the outset. That is, by starting a venture that at least has the potential to make you seriously rich rather than just seriously busy. Being busy is the ultimate goal of managers and bureaucrats rather than of entrepreneurs.

Neither does the formula give you 'the answer to everything'. Launching the right business is an essential first step to wealth creation, but though necessary it is not sufficient on its own. A business plan has to be written, money raised, markets entered and management teams built and motivated. The business has to be sold, wholly or partially, and the money banked. Until that point any value created is purely notional, which, though in itself a comfort, is not yours to spend as you will. Finally, you need to find something to do with the rest of your life, other than play golf or sail your yacht. Unfortunately, the characteristics of successful entrepreneurs include a low boredom threshold and the need to be involved in new challenges. These are all topics addressed in later chapters of this book.

IF AT FIRST YOU DON'T SUCCEED

If you are one of the tens of millions of people already running their own business and have discovered that you are running the wrong business or can see that you are not on track to creating serious value, don't despair. Just because you got the formula wrong this time doesn't mean you won't go on to greater things. Henry Ford had a couple of shots at business before he got his value formula right. Milton Hershey started three unsuccessful candy companies in Philadelphia, Chicago and New York before founding the Hershey Company, which brought milk chocolate – previously a Swiss delicacy – to the masses. Walt Disney's first business, Laugh-O-Gram, was so unsuccessful that at one point he resorted to eating dog food to stay alive. Thomas Edison filed 1093 patents, mostly for unsuccessful ventures, before striking gold with the light bulb. His statement 'I have not failed. I've just found 10,000 ways that won't work' is the stuff of legend.

THE FAILURE MYTH

Another useful fact to know is that the rumour of calamities awaiting most new ventures is just that – an unfounded and incorrect piece of oft-repeated misinformation. An exhaustive study of the eight-year destinations of all 814,000 US firms founded in a particular year by Bruce A. Kirchoff, professor of management at New Jersey Institute of Technology, revealed that just 18 per cent actually failed, meaning that the entrepreneurs were put out of business by their financial backers, lack of demand or competitive pressures. True, some 28 per cent of businesses closed their doors voluntarily, their founders having decided for a variety of reasons that either working for themselves or this particular type of business was just not for them. But the majority of the businesses studied in Kirchoff's mammoth and representative study survived and in many cases prospered.

With a degree of preparation, a fair amount of perspiration and a modicum of luck you can get started and may even, as in many of the case examples described throughout this book, end up with a substantial, successful and growing enterprise. To begin well, as they say, is to end well. Read on.

Chapter 2

The traits of the entrepreneur – it's all in the mindset

ENTREPRENEUR vs SMALL BUSINESS OWNER

The terms 'entrepreneur' and 'small business owner' are often used interchangeably in the lexicon of commerce, but there are some very real differences between the two groups.

It was eighteenth-century French economist Jean-Baptiste Say who first coined the term entrepreneur as a means of distinguishing between the majority of people owning and running small businesses and the smaller but much more important group who contributed significantly to the well-being of economies at large. As he defined it, an entrepreneur could be characterised as a creative, risk-taking forecaster: someone who projected and appraised future opportunities. In his view, 'an entrepreneur possessed the moral qualities of judgment and perseverance, while also having knowledge of the world'.

To some extent you could say the same about anyone who starts and runs a company and it's true that entrepreneurs and other business people have some traits in common. However, not everyone will take a business and grow from relatively small beginnings into a multimillion-pound enterprise. That tends to be the province of those with an entrepreneurial approach to commerce. But what does that mean in practice?

VISIONARIES AND LEADERS

The first thing that has to be said is that ambition and vision are hugely important. For instance, Bill Gates, Microsoft's founder, stated from the outset that he wanted to see a computer in every home when barely a handful of major offices had one. It was only a decade earlier that IBM had estimated the entire world demand for its computers as seven! Apple Computer's founder, Steve Jobs, wanted to make computers 'fun' in an era when DOS prevailed and the whole subject of business was serious. Exploiting the mouse and the graphical user interface (GUI), Jobs found a way to get information into a computer that was both intuitive and fun for users. Neither of these were his inventions, but like many entrepreneurs, he recognised an opportunity when he spotted it.

But the approach isn't simply about vision. Entrepreneurs can only release value if they can both lead and manage. Dozens of catchy terms such as bottom up, top down, management by objectives and crisis management have been used to describe the many and various theories on how to manage. There is no single way to lead and manage a company and much will depend on the owner's personality and style. However, what you are aiming to create is a situation where you can harness the skills of others to achieve your goals. That means working towards building a team of motivated people. We'll be looking at this in detail later in the book.

THE ENTREPRENEUR AS INNOVATOR AND CREATIVE DESTROYER

Entrepreneurs may not always be first to market with a new invention or technology, as we saw in Chapter 1, but inevitably they are innovators, a word that embodies both the creation of new models and ways of doing things along with the destruction of the old.

Creative destruction is a term attributed to Joseph Schumpeter. Born in 1883, at 26 he became the youngest professor in the Austrian empire and finance minister at 36, only to be dismissed after presiding over a period of hyperinflation. A brief spell as president of a small Viennese bank was followed, after its failure, by a return to academia, first in Bonn then in 1932 at Harvard. He is remembered for two books in particular, *The Theory of Economic Development* (1911), where he first outlined his thoughts on entrepreneurship, and *Capitalism, Socialism and Democracy* (1942), in which he detailed how the entrepreneurial process worked and why it mattered. His view was that the fundamental impulse that sets and keeps the capitalist engine in motion comes from 'the new consumers, goods, the new methods of production or transportation, the new markets, the new forms of industrial organization that capitalist enterprise creates'. He pointed out that entrepreneurs innovate and develop new products, services or ways of doing business, and in the process destroy those organisations that can't adapt or that have effectively been made redundant.

Schumpeter believed that capitalism has to create short-term losers alongside its short- and long-term winners in order for the economy to grow and prosper: 'Without innovations, no entrepreneurs; without entrepreneurial achievement, no capitalist ... propulsion. The atmosphere of industrial revolutions... is the only one in which capitalism can survive.' He went rather further than this by arguing that the more countries tried to mitigate the possibilities of business failing, the worse their economic performance would be. Picking up the pieces through social insurance is fine; propping up failing businesses or declining business sectors is not. Perhaps it's just as well that he was not around to see the Northern Rock, Bear Stearns or AIG bailouts.

ACCEPTANCE OF UNCERTAINTY

Managers in big businesses set out to minimise risk by delaying decisions until every possible fact is known. This response to uncertainty is one that challenges the need to operate in the unknown. There is a feeling that to work without all the facts is not prudent or desirable. Entrepreneurs, on the other hand, know that by the time the fog of uncertainty has been completely lifted, too many people will be able to spot the opportunity clearly. In fact, an entrepreneur would usually only be interested in a decision that involved accepting a degree of uncertainty and would welcome, and on occasion even relish, that position. An essential characteristic of an entrepreneur is the willingness to make decisions and to take risks. There is a less useful side effect to this willingness to take risks, however.

Entrepreneurs are deluded – Official

University researchers at the Fisher College of Business, Ohio State University, tested the decision-making processes of 124 entrepreneurs and 95 managers at big companies by asking a number of questions. First, they asked five general questions with two parts to each: the first part with only two possible answers (e.g. which causes more deaths: cancer or heart disease?), the second asking respondents their level of confidence in the answer, from 50 per cent (guessing) to 100 per cent (completely sure).

Secondly, the researchers asked a question about management decisions. For example:

Some equipment has broken down and you have to replace it. The options are:

1. Buy an American-made machine. A friend recently purchased this machine and hasn't had problems with it.
2. Buy an imported machine, which statistics show has a lower chance of problems than its American-made counterpart.

The results showed that about half of the entrepreneurs chose the American-made product while 90 per cent of the managers chose the imported model.

The study yielded two conclusions:

1. Entrepreneurs are much more confident that they are right – especially when they are wrong.
2. Entrepreneurs prefer hunches to data.

Confident and optimistic people – one way of describing entrepreneurs – look at the probability of success, while cautious conservative people – managers – look at the probability of failure. The confident type is likely to take a part as representative of the whole, possibly making a decision blindly. The challenge for entrepreneurs is to accept uncertainty knowing that they could be swept away in a maelstrom of creative destruction. They do have a scrap of comfort, nevertheless. The limited liability laws let business people protect personal assets and put some parameters on the level of downside they are prepared to accept.

OTHER TYPES OF ENTREPRENEUR

There are many other traits that entrepreneurs share: the capacity for hard work, good all-round business skills, discontent with the way things are currently being done and the capacity to think big, to mention but a few. However, not every entrepreneur fits neatly into the mould of a full-blooded creative visionary operating in an environment of their own making. There are some other types of entrepreneur who by virtue of their peculiar circumstances can either dispense with some of the above characteristics or at any rate exhibit them to a lesser degree. These include the following.

Social entrepreneurs
Social entrepreneurs are concerned primarily with achieving sustainable social change, a branch of entrepreneurship that is fast becoming mainstream. There is an annual Queen's Award for Industry for Sustainable Development, an ACCA Award for the Best Social Accounts and a School for Social Entrepreneurs (www.sse.org.uk) that helps would-be social entrepreneurs to get

started. The Schwab Foundation (www.schwabfound.org) covers much the same ground in the US.

According to government statistics, around 55,000 businesses trade with a social or environmental purpose across the UK. They contribute almost £27 billion to the national economy and substantially benefit their local communities by creating employment opportunities, providing ethical products and services, and reinvesting surpluses into society. The primary motivation for social entrepreneurs is to build an ethical venture that is of benefit to the wider community. As one social entrepreneur put it, 'I am trying to build a little part of the world in which I would like to live.' Money is important, but getting rich is not.

Oneworld Health (www.oneworldhealth.org) – an agent of positive change

Established by Victoria Hale, a social entrepreneur and pharmacologist based in San Francisco, Oneworld Health is as different from mainstream drug companies as it is possible to be. It has as its vision to 'serve as a positive agent for change by saving lives, improving health, and fulfilling the promise of medicine for those most in need' and for its values 'Integrity, Courage, Collaboration'. Oneworld assembles experienced and dedicated teams of pharmaceutical scientists to identify the most promising drugs and vaccine candidates and develops them into safe, effective and affordable medicines. Then it partners with companies, not-for-profit hospitals and organisations in the developing world to conduct medical research on new cures. Oneworld manufactures and distributes newly approved therapies such as those that tackle malaria, the cause of 300–500 million acute illnesses and over 1 million deaths annually.

> The company scours the virtual shelves of big phar-
> maceutical companies looking for drugs that for some
> reason failed to get to market, perhaps because the
> market proved too small, the benefits too few or in
> some other way they didn't meet the needs of an
> affluent western market. Hale even persuaded the
> University of California Santa Barbara to donate a
> patent for a discovery involving the novel use of calcium
> channel blockers to control the schistosomiasis para-
> site. Hale and her team believe that there are huge
> inefficiencies in the way drugs are currently devised
> and produced in the western world and have secured
> $140 million from the Bill and Melinda Gates Foundation
> to help in their work.

Intrapreneurs

The Economist of 25 December 1976 carried a survey called 'The
coming entrepreneurial revolution', in which Norman Macrae,
the magazine's deputy editor, contended that 'methods of operation in business were going to change radically in the next few
decades'. The world, Macrae argued, was probably drawing to
the end of the era of big business corporations; it would soon
be nonsense to have hierarchical managements sitting in sky-
scrapers trying to arrange how brainworkers (who in future
would be most workers) could best use their imaginations. The
main increases in employment would henceforth come either in
small firms or in those bigger firms that managed to split themselves into smaller and smaller profit centres that in turn would
need to become more and more entrepreneurial.

Two years later, Gifford Pinchot III and his wife Elizabeth
S. Pinchot founded Pinchot & Company (www.pinchot.com),
an organisation based around the proposition that you don't

have to leave the corporation to become an entrepreneur. They advanced the idea that the way for big business to adapt was to create an environment where managers could behave as though they were entrepreneurs, but within the business using its resources. By 1992 the term intrapreneur had been added to the third edition of *The American Dictionary of the English Language.*

Unlike entrepreneurs, intrapreneurs don't have 'doing their own thing' at the top of their list of motivators. They feel happier in a comfort zone afforded by a corporate structure and with the resources and respectability that provides.

Buy-out Entrepreneurs

We will look at these in more detail in Chapter 13, when ways to realise value are examined. In brief, an MBO (management buy-out) occurs when some or all of the incumbent team buy out the founder); and an MBI (management buy-in) occurs when a venture capital firm shoehorns in its own pre-ferred managing director, easing the incumbent founder out and oiling the wheels with some additional investment. A BIMBO (buy-in management buy-out) is a combination of the two. Often a buy-out can release a surge of entrepreneurial energy, something that is certainly encouraged by the private equity investment houses that are enthusiastic backers of these deals.

More than one way

The moral is that there is certainly more than one context in which to harness the entrepreneurial spirit. Many entrepreneurs are fiercely independent, while others have many of the same instincts but are content to work with or within much larger organisations. Another group find their independence and entrepreneurial spirit through a buy-out. And as social entrepreneurs demonstrate, money isn't always everything.

This book is focused on those who start and grow their businesses themselves, but that certainly isn't the only route to success.

Chapter 3

Nothing new under the sun – the same old problems, some brand new solutions

The prerequisite for business success is an ability to sell products and services, but clearly this is something that some companies do much more successfully than others. Think of it this way. You have two identical businesses offering similar wares. One enjoys steady sales but struggles to reach beyond a core market, the other clocks up double-digit growth year on year and somehow seems to capture the imagination and spending power of an ever-expanding constituency.

Indeed, when you think of the iconic entrepreneurial success stories of recent times, the common factor is the ability of the founders to do more than sell quality products to a pre-defined market. From Bill Gates and his vision of a PC in every home to Anita Roddick and her mission to carve out a market for ethical beauty products, we can see how entrepreneurs often tap into latent demand that barely registers on the radar screens of other companies.

To do this successfully requires more than vision. It needs a real understanding of customer need and the principles of modern marketing.

KNOWING THE CUSTOMER

The phrase 'the customer is king' may be overworked, but it holds the key to business success. Once upon a time customers were simply sold products and the focus of innovative businesses lay in driving costs down in order to widen and open up as big a market as possible. Henry Ford's much quoted 'you can have any color as long as it's black' was part of a determined and successful strategy to build a car for the masses. There is no evidence that Ford actually said those words, but from 1908 to 1927 the Model T, assembled at the Piquette Avenue Plant in Detroit, churned out 15 million vehicles with little change in its design. This was the longest run of any single model apart from the Volkswagen Beetle.

The change in emphasis from selling on price to marketing was captured in the classic *Harvard Business Review* article 'Marketing myopia' by Theodore Levitt, published in 1960.

Levitt, who died in 2006, produced a score of other thoughtful articles but none that outsold the 850,000 reprints to which this one ran. The thrust of his proposition was that the difference between marketing and selling is more than semantic. Selling, he claimed, focuses on the needs of the seller, marketing on the needs of the buyer. Selling is preoccupied with the seller's need to convert the product into cash, marketing with the idea of satisfying the needs of the customer by means of the product and the whole cluster of things associated with creating, delivering and, finally, consuming it. Levitt went on to argue that in some industries, the enticements of full mass production have been so powerful that top management in effect has told the sales department, 'You get rid of it; we'll worry about profits'. By contrast, a truly marketing-minded firm tries to create value-satisfying goods and services that satisfy consumers' needs.

The benefit Levitt saw for businesses was that needs endure, while products come and go. He used the railroad as an example of a business that had defined itself too narrowly. At the turn of the twentieth century American railroads enjoyed a fierce loyalty among astute US investors and European monarchs plunged in too. The prevailing view was that eternal wealth was assured and no other form of transportation could compete with the railroads in speed, flexibility, durability, economy and growth potential. Even when cars, lorries and aeroplanes arrived, the railroad tycoons remained unconcerned. If you had told them that in a few short decades they would be broke and pleading for government subsidies, they would have thought you totally demented. Yet that's what happened and, as Levitt argued, it did not come about primarily because of a fundamental change. After all, people still travelled and goods were distributed, it was just that these needs were satisfied by other means. (You can download a reprint of the 'Marketing myopia' article free at www.dallascap.com.)

THE MARKETING MISSION AND WHY IT MATTERS

Marketing is defined as the process that ensures that the right products and services get to the right markets at the right time and at the right price. You have to offer value and satisfaction otherwise people will either choose an apparently superior competitor, or if they do buy from you and are dissatisfied they won't buy again; worse still, they may bad mouth you to a whole mass of other people. Being right means that there have to be enough people wanting your product or service to make the venture profitable; and ideally those numbers should be getting bigger rather than smaller.

The boundaries of marketing stretch from inside the mind of the customer, perhaps uncovering emotions they were themselves barely aware of, out to the logistic support systems that get the product or service into customers' hands. Each part of the value chain from company to consumer has the potential to add value or kill the deal. For example, at the heart of Amazon's business proposition are a superlatively efficient warehousing and delivery system and a simple, zero-cost way for customers to return products they don't want and get immediate refunds. These factors are every bit as important as elements of Amazon's marketing strategy as are its product range, website structure, Google placement or competitive pricing.

Missions Turn Business Ideas into Money-Generating Propositions

Marketing is turned from a theoretical concept into a practical, money-generating activity by virtue of a mission. This is a statement with two key attributes. First, the mission should be narrow enough to give direction and guidance to everything you do or plan to do. This concentration is the key to business success, because it is only by focusing on specific needs that a business can differentiate itself from established competitors. Second, the mission should open up a large enough market to allow the business to grow, realise its potential and make lots of money. Above all, mission statements must be realistic, achievable – and brief.

The mission has to resonate inside the business as well as in the marketplace. For example, financial services company Lehman Brothers' mission included the message 'We are one firm', a sentiment that didn't carry much weight when the chips were down in September 2008. All the cash was transmitted from the London branch to the New York HQ, leaving UK employees temporarily stranded.

Blooming Marvellous – building on a mission statement

Judy Lever and Vivienne Pringle started Blooming Marvellous literally on a kitchen table back in 1983. Both were pregnant and after searching for the kind of fashionable clothes they used to wear and drawing a blank, they guessed they had found a gap in the market. Their mission, developed on a business start-up course, stated: 'Arising out of our experiences, we intend to design, make and market a range of clothes for mothers-to-be that will make them feel they can still be fashionably dressed. We aim to serve a niche missed out by Mothercare and Marks & Spencer, and so become a significant force in the mail order fashion for the mothers-to-be market.'

The two kept their day jobs and would meet after work every day at Judy's house to answer enquiries, send out leaflets and dispatch products in the post every day. They outsourced work to a pattern cutter, a small factory, some fabric suppliers, and eventually to a small distribution centre. After a year or so of modest sales, they felt confident enough to set up their first business premises: a 1200 sq ft warehouse on a business park staffed by four of the women who had been working in their distribution centre.

The company now employs 150 people, has 14 shops and has extended its range to include nursery products, toys, themed bedroom accessories and a separate brand called Mini Marvellous that caters for children aged 2–8 years.

FULFILLING CUSTOMER NEED

The founder of a successful cosmetics firm, when asked what he did, replied: 'In the factories we make perfume. In the shops we sell dreams.' Business founders usually start out defining their business in physical terms. Customers, on the other hand, see the primary value of a business as having the ability to satisfy their needs. Even firms that adopt customer satisfaction, or even delight, as their stated maxim often find it a more complex goal than it at first appears. Take Blooming Marvellous by way of an example. It makes clothes for mothers-to-be, sure enough, but the primary customer need it was aiming to satisfy was not either to preserve their modesty or to keep them warm. The need they were aiming for was much higher: they were trying to ensure that their customers would feel fashionably dressed, which is about the way people interact with each other and how they feel about themselves. Just splashing on, say, a tog rating showing the thermal properties of the fabric, as you would with a duvet, would cut no ice with Blooming Marvellous's potential market.

Though needs are enduring – and had the investors in railways understood them better they may have kept their fortunes – understanding those needs is not always easy. Fortunately, help is at hand. American psychologist Abraham Maslow demonstrated in his research that 'all customers are goal seekers who gratify their needs by purchase and consumption'. In his 1943 paper 'A theory of human motivation', he went somewhat further and classified consumer needs into a pyramid he called the hierarchy of needs, with more basic needs at the bottom, rising to higher ones as the earlier needs were met. Maslow's research was not specifically related to business. He studied what he called exemplary people such as Albert Einstein, Eleanor Roosevelt and the brightest of his students, rather than the mentally ill or neurotic people who interested others in the field such as Sigmund Freud. Maslow's view was that 'the study of crippled, stunted, immature, and unhealthy specimens can yield only a cripple psychology and a cripple philosophy'. His hierarchy can be broken down as follows:

Physiological needs: Air, water, sleep and food are all absolutely essential to sustain life. Until these basic needs are satisfied, higher needs such as self-esteem will not even be considered.

Safety needs: The second most basic need of consumers is to feel safe and secure. People who feel that they are at risk of harm, either through their general environment or because of the product or service on offer, will not be overinterested in having their higher needs met. When Charles Rigby set up World Challenge (www.world-challenge.co.uk) to market challenging expeditions to exotic locations around the world, with the aim of taking young people up to the age of 19 out of their comfort zone and teaching them how to overcome adversity, he knew he had a challenge of his own on his hands: how to make an activity simultaneously exciting and apparently dangerous to teenagers, while being safe enough for the parents writing the cheques to feel comfortable. Six full sections on the company's website are devoted to explaining the safety measures it takes to ensure that unacceptable risks are eliminated as far as is humanly possible.

Social needs: The need for friends, belonging to associations, clubs or other groups and the need to give and get love are all social needs. After 'lower' needs have been met these needs that relate to interacting with other people come to the fore. Hotel Chocolat (www.hotelchocolat.co.uk), founded by Angus Thirlwell and Peter Harris in their kitchen, is a good example of a business based on meeting social needs. They market luxury chocolates, but generate sales by having Tasting Clubs to check out products each month. The concept of the club is that you invite friends round and use the firm's scoring system to rate and give feedback on the chocolates.

Esteem needs: Here people are concerned with such matters as self-respect, achievement, attention, recognition and reputation. The benefits customers are looking for at this level include the feeling that others will think better of them if they have a particular product. Much brand marketing is aimed at making consumers believe that conspicuously wearing the maker's label or logo so that others can see it will earn them 'respect'. Understanding how this part of Maslow's hierarchy works was vital to the founders of Responsibletravel.com (www.responsibletravel.com). Founded six years ago with backing from The Body Shop's Anita Roddick in a front room in Brighton, Justin Francis and his partner Harold Goodwin set out to be the world's first company to offer environmentally responsible travel and holidays. They were one of the first companies to offer carbon offset schemes for travellers and they boast that they turn away more tour companies trying to list on their site than they accept. They appeal to consumers who want to be recognised in their community as being socially responsible.

Self-actualisation: This is the summit of Maslow's hierarchy in which people are looking for truth, wisdom, justice and purpose. It is a need that is never fully satisfied and according to Maslow, only a very small percentage of people ever reach the point where they are prepared to pay much money to satisfy such needs. It is left to the likes of Bill Gates and Sir Tom Hunter to give away billions forming foundations to dispose of their wealth on worthy causes. The rest of us scrabble around further down the hierarchy.

You can read more about Maslow's hierarchy of needs and how to take it into account in understanding customers on the Net MBA website (www.netmba.com).

BENEFIT CULTURE – WHAT'S IN IT FOR THE CUSTOMER?

While understanding customer needs is vital, it is not sufficient on its own to help put together a saleable proposition. Before you can do that you have to understand the benefits that customers will get when they purchase what you are offering. *Features* are what a product or service has or is, and *benefits* are what the product or service does for the customer. When Nigel Apperley founded his business Internet Cameras Direct, now Internet Direct (www.internetdirect.co.uk), while a student at business school, he knew that there was no point telling customers about SLRs or shutter speeds. These are not the end needs that customers want satisfying; they are looking for the convenience and economy of buying direct as well as good pictures. Apperley planned to follow the Dell Computer direct sales model. Within three years he had an annual turnover in excess of £20 million and had realised much of the value of his business by becoming part of the AIM-listed eXpansy plc.

GENERIC MARKETING STRATEGIES

You might be forgiven for believing that there are millions of strategies for meeting customer needs. In fact, while there are certainly lots of variations, there are only three serious options. Credit for devising the most succinct and usable way to get a handle on the big picture has to be given to Michael E. Porter, who trained as an economist at Princeton, gaining an MBA (1971) and a PhD (1973) at Harvard Business School. His book *Competitive Strategy: Techniques for Analyzing Industries and Competitors* sets out the now accepted methodology for devising strategy.

Porter's first observation was that two factors above all influenced a business's chances of making superior profits. The first was the attractiveness or otherwise of the industry in which it primarily operated. Second, and in terms of an organisation's sphere of influence more important, was how the business positioned itself within that industry. In that respect a business could only have a cost advantage in that it could make products or deliver services for less than others, or in that it could differentiate itself in a way that mattered to consumers, so that its offers would be unique, or at least relatively so. Porter added a further twist to his prescription. Businesses could follow either a cost advantage path or a differentiation path industry wide, or they could take a third path – they could concentrate on a narrow specific segment, either with cost advantage or differentiation. This he termed a focus strategy.

Cost Leadership

Low cost should not be confused with low price. A business with low costs may or may not pass the savings it makes on to customers. Alternatively, it could use that position alongside tight cost controls and low margins to create an effective barrier to others considering either entering or extending their penetration of that market. Low cost strategies are most likely to be achievable in large markets, requiring large-scale capital investment, where production or service volumes are high and economies of scale can be achieved from long runs.

Low costs are not a lucky accident, they can be achieved through these main activities:

Operating efficiencies: These can be achieved by new processes, methods of working or less costly ways of working. Ryanair and easyJet are examples of businesses where analysing every component of the business made it possible to strip out major elements of cost.

Product redesign: This involves fundamentally rethinking a product or service proposition to look for more efficient ways to work or cheaper substitute materials to work with. The motor industry has adopted this approach with 'platform sharing', where major players including Citroën, Peugeot and Toyota have rethought their entry car models to share major components.

Product standardisation: Having a wide range of product and service offers claiming to extend customer choice invariably leads to higher costs. The challenge is being sure that proliferation gives real choice and adds value. In 2008 the UK railway network took a long, hard look at its dozens of different fare structures and scores of names, often for identical price structures, which had remained largely unchanged since the 1960s, and reduced them to three basic product propositions. Adopting this and other common standards across the rail network should substantially reduce the currently excessive £500 million transaction cost of selling £5 billion worth of tickets.

Economies of scale: Such economies can be achieved only by being big or bold. The same head office, warehousing network and distribution chain can support Tesco's 3263 stores as the 997 that Somerfield has. The former will have a lower cost base by virtue of having more outlets to spread its costs over, as well as having more purchasing power. Lloyds TSB expects to generate £1 billion of extra profit from its shotgun marriage to HBOS, by merging networks and back-office staff and systemsm and it will need to.

EasyJet – success through cost leadership

You'd have to be a bit crazy to think seriously about competing in the airline industry today, because the dice are loaded against airlines as money-making propositions. The fixed costs of doing business are extremely high, so nearly everything an airline does has to be paid for in advance, before a single passenger coughs up and boards a plane. In addition, there's hardly any brand loyalty in airline travel. Throw in the fickleness of the weather, and what you have is a recipe for disaster rather than profits.

None of these problems fazed Stelios Haji-Ioannou, who founded easyJet in 1995. The airline's inaugural flights from London Luton to Edinburgh and Glasgow were supported by an advertising campaign headlined 'Making flying as affordable as a pair of jeans – £29 one way'. At this time, the airline had two leased Boeing 737-200 aircraft and essentially acted as a 'virtual airline', contracting in everything from pilots to check-in staff. Early on, Stelios (always known by his first name) came to the conclusion that many passengers just want to get from point A to point B at the lowest possible price, so he started an airline without frills. easyJet offers no commissions to travel agents and has even eliminated meals during flights. The company was also quick to take advantage of Internet reservations and ticketless travel to reduce costs even further.

However, the real savings at easyJet are in turn-around time. Stelios realised early on that the key to profits is keeping planes in the air, so he came up with a new way to operate. easyJet flies only short-haul routes and the company uses just one type of aircraft to minimise parts inventory, training and maintenance costs — and to reduce downtime.

easyJet has been selected as a Business Superbrand by the Superbrand Council, which recognises companies with an outstanding brand name. Other Superbrand companies include such globally recognised names as Virgin, Coca-Cola and Manchester United. In addition, *Marketing* magazine described the launch of easyJet as 'one of the 100 great marketing moments of the 20th century'. Nevertheless, despite his much-deserved success Stelios was doing nothing new. Southwest Airlines, started by Rollin King and Herb Kelleher two decades earlier, uses the same business model and dozens more have followed in their wake.

Standing out – principles of differentiation

The key to a differentiation strategy is a deep understanding of what customers really want and need and, more importantly, what they are prepared to pay more for. Apple's opening strategy was based around a 'fun' operating system based on icons, rather than the dull MS-DOS. This belief was based on its founders understanding that computer users were mostly young and wanted an intuitive command system; the graphical user interface delivered just that. Apple has continued its differentiation strategy, but added design and fashion to ease of control to the ways in which it delivers extra value. Sony and BMW are also examples of differentiators. Both benefit from distinctive and desirable differences in their products. None of these companies offers the lowest price in their respective industries; customers are willing to pay extra for the idiosyncratic and prized differences embedded in their products.

Differentiation doesn't have to be confined to the marketing arena, nor does it always lead to success if the subject of that differentiation disappears without much warning. Northern Rock, a failed bank that had to be nationalised to keep it in business, thought that its strategy of raising most of the money it lent out in mortgages through the money markets was a sure winner. This allowed the bank to grow faster than its competitors, which placed more reliance on depositors for their funds. As long as interest rates were low and the money market functioned smoothly, the strategy worked. But once the differentiators that fuelled Northern Rock's growth were reversed, its business model failed.

Focusing your business

A focus strategy involves concentrating on serving a particular market or a defined geographic region. Furniture company IKEA, for example, targets young, white-collar workers as its prime customer segment, selling through 235 stores in more than 30 countries. Ingvar Kamprad, an entrepreneur from the Småland province in southern Sweden who founded the business in the late 1940s, offers home furnishing products of good function and design at prices young people can afford. He achieves this by using simple cost-cutting solutions that do not affect the quality of the products.

Warren Buffett, the world's richest man who knows a thing or two about focus, combined with confectionary company Mars to buy US chewing gum manufacturer Wrigley for $23 billion (£11.6 billion) in 2008. Chicago-based Wrigley, which launched its Spearmint and Juicy Fruit gums in the 1890s, specialises in chewing gum and has consistently outperformed its more diversified competitors. It is the only major consumer products company to grow comfortably faster than the population in its markets and above the rate of inflation. Over the past decade or so, other consumer products companies have diversified. Gillette moved into supplying the batteries used to drive many of its products by acquiring Duracell. Nestlé bought food companies Ralston Purina, Dreyer's, Ice Cream Partners and Chef America. Nevertheless, both have trailed Wrigley's performance.

Businesses often lose their focus over time and periodically have to rediscover their core strategic purpose. Procter & Gamble is an example of a business that had to refocus to cure weak growth. In 2000 the company was losing share in seven of its top nine categories, and had lowered earnings expectations four times in two quarters. This prompted the company to restructure and refocus on its core business: big brands, big customers and big countries. It sold off non-core businesses, establishing five global business units with a closely focused product portfolio.

THE FIVE FORCES THAT DRIVE COMPETITION

Aside from articulating the generic approach to business strategy, Porter's other major contribution to the field of strategy is what has become known as the five forces theory of industry structure. Porter postulated that the five forces that drive competition in an industry have to be understood as part of a process of choosing which of the three generic strategies to pursue. The forces he identified are:

1. *Threat of substitution:* Can customers buy something else instead of your product? For example, Apple and to a lesser extent Sony produce laptop computers that are distinctive enough to make substitution difficult. Dell, on the other hand, faces intense competition from dozens of other suppliers with near identical products competing mostly on price alone.
2. *Threat of new entrants:* If it is easy to enter your market, start-up costs are low and there are no barriers to entry such as IP (intellectual property) protection, then the threat of new entrants is high.
3. *Supplier power:* The fewer the suppliers, usually the more powerful they are. Oil is a classic example, where fewer than a dozen countries supply the whole market and consequently can set prices.
4. *Buyer power:* In the food market for example, just a few, powerful supermarket buyers are supplied by thousands of much smaller businesses and are often able to dictate terms.
5. *Industry competition:* The number and capability of competitors form one determinant of a business's power. Having few competitors with relatively less attractive products or services lowers the intensity of rivalry in a sector. Often such sectors slip into oligopolistic behaviour where the small number of big players prefer to collude rather than compete.

So there's a lot to get to grips with. In order to trade successfully you will need to have an intimate knowledge of your customers – their needs and desires – plus a solid awareness of the market forces that affect your company's ability to sell. Research is therefore vital, and that's what we'll be looking at in the next chapter.

Chapter 4

Research, research, research

THE EDGE – SHOWING INVESTORS YOU KNOW MORE THAN THEY DO

Getting a new venture off the ground and growing it to the point where it is truly valuable will bring you into contact with a lot of clever, knowledgeable people. Venture capital firms, the biggest backers of risky propositions, are crammed full of MBA researchers and if they don't have the right knowledge they are not shy of buying it in. They are also extremely picky. Worldwide, venture capitalists invest in around 10,000 businesses each year. In the UK, for example, the 214 members of the British Venture Capital Association put cash into just 1680 ventures in 2007/8, and that was a fairly typical year. That's about seven deals a year per venture capitalist, which doesn't exactly appear to make them overworked. However, they do see around 1000 business plans for each business they back, and they research in some considerable detail about a dozen of those.

It is also a fact that most venture capitalists, business angels and corporate venture funders focus on a particular market sector or technology. One firm, for example, specialises in mining, with teams dedicated to sub-sectors such as coal, diamonds, gold and platinum. Another covers the travel and leisure fields, breaking that down to airlines, gambling, hotels, recreational activities and restaurants and bars.

This is where you have the advantage, as much of their knowledge may be dated and general. For example, let's say that you're launching a business supplying the hotel trade. Potential investors will know, from published research, hotel occupancy rates and average room costs, broken down by category and region for the past few years. What they will not know is how much money is spent on toiletry products per bed night, who currently supplies hotels with these products, how much they pay, what the profit margins are, how satisfied the hotel's customers are with those products and what their preferences would be if they were given a choice. That's the kind of detail that potential investors long to hear.

There is a sting in the tail in the knowledge game. Investors and bankers, partners, suppliers, even potential landlords may not have detailed information on all the factors that will eventually determine whether your startup or growth plans make sense. But the chances are that they have a lot of experience in asking probing questions. Fortunately, these questions are all the ones you need answers to as well.

THE BASICS OF BUSINESS RESEARCH

You don't have to launch a product or enter a market to prove that there are no customers for your goods or services; frequently even some modest market research beforehand can give clear guidance as to whether your venture will succeed or not. While big businesses may employ market research agencies to design and execute their research, an entrepreneur should both understand the process and be able to carry out elementary research quickly and on a low budget.

Your business research has two goals. The first is to build credibility for your business proposition and to be able to demonstrate – initially to your own satisfaction, and later to colleagues, collaborators and eventually to financiers – a thorough understanding of the marketplace for the new product, service or strategy. This will be vital if you are to attract the resources to execute the proposal.

The second is to develop a realistic market entry strategy for the proposed course of action, based on a clear understanding of genuine customer needs, and to ensure that product quality, price, promotional methods and the distribution chain are mutually supportive and clearly focused on target customers. As a minimum you need to know more about these areas that does anyone to whom you are looking for support for your business. If they can catch you out they will – and if they do your credibility is blown, as are your chances of enlisting them to your cause.

What to research

- Your customers – who will buy your goods and services? What particular customer needs will your business meet? How many of them are there?
- Your competitors – which established companies are already meeting or attempting to meet the needs of your potential customers? What are their strengths and weaknesses?
- Your product or service – how should it be tailored to meet customer needs?

- What price should you charge to be perceived as giving value for money?
- What promotional material is needed to reach customers; which newspapers, journals do they read?
- Is your operational base satisfactorily located to reach your customers most easily, at minimum cost?

The third goal of research is to identify the scale and nature of the risks inherent in the venture. Financiers will always ask a question along the lines of 'What do you think could go wrong?' or 'Why did the last business in your sector fail?'. These are all risk-probing questions. The true entrepreneur only takes calculated risks.

Freddie Laker, who started the first low-cost, no-frills airline, bet everything he could raise on buying more planes than he could afford. To compound the risk he bet against the exchange rate between the pound and the dollar, and lost. His business was leveraged (see Chapter 6 for more on this) at £258 of borrowings for every £1 of his own capital, so when things went wrong he sank without trace.

Laker also broke a taboo: he took on the big boys on their own ground. He upset the British and American national carriers on their most lucrative routes. There was no way that big, entrenched businesses with deep pockets would yield territory to a newcomer without a fight to the death.

That's not to say that Laker's business model was wrong; after all, RyanAir and easyJet have proved it can work. But those businesses tackled the short-haul market to and from new airfields, and in the case of easyJet at least started out with tens of millions of pounds of family money that came from a lifetime in the transportation business.

THE SEVEN STEPS TO SUPERIOR BUSINESS KNOWLEDGE

Business research is certainly not rocket science and it doesn't have to cost an arm and a leg to carry out. The amount of effort and expenditure needs to be related in some way to the costs and risks associated with the proposition. Procter & Gamble, for example, test marketed the home dry-cleaning product Dryel in 150,000 households for more than three years before introducing the product. But it was proposing a substantial seven- or eight-figure investment and its brand name was on the line too. Your business research needs to be conducted professionally if it is to be credible. Systematically following these seven steps will keep you on the right track:

1. *Formulate the problem:* Before embarking on any research, you should first set clear and precise objectives, rather than just setting out to find interesting general information about the market. So, for example, if you are planning on selling to young, fashion-conscious women, your research objective could be to find out how many women aged 18 to 28, with an income of over £35,000 a year, live or work within your catchment area. That would give you some idea of whether the market could support a venture such as this.

2. *Determine the information needs:* Knowing the size of the market, in the example given above, may require several different pieces of information. You would need to know the size of the resident population, which might be fairly easy to find out, but you might also want to know something about people who come into the catchment area to work or stay on holiday or for any other major purpose. There might, for example, be a hospital, library, railway station or school nearby that also pulls potential customers to the area.

3. *Consider where you can get the information:* This will involve either desk research in libraries or on the Internet, or field research, which you can do yourself or get help in doing. Field research – that is, getting out and asking questions yourself – is the most fruitful way of gathering original information that can provide competitive advantage. It is also knowledge that an investor is unlikely to have and will value greatly.

4. *Decide on the budget:* Research will not be free, even if you do it yourself. At the very least there will be the cost of your time. There may well be the cost of journals, phone calls, letters and field visits to plan for. At the top of the scale could be the costs of employing a professional market research firm. Starting at this end of the scale, a business-to-business survey comprising 200 interviews with executives responsible for office equipment purchasing decisions cost one company £12,000; 20 in-depth interviews with consumers who are regular users of certain banking services cost £8000. Using the Internet for surveys is another possibility, but that can impose too much of your agenda on the recipients and turn them away from you. Check out companies such as Free Online Surveys (http://free-online-surveys.co.uk) and Zoomerang (www.zoomerang.com), which provide software that lets you carry out online surveys and analyse the data quickly. Most of these organisations offer free trials.

Doing the research yourself may save costs but may limit the objectivity of the research. If time is your scarcest commodity, it may make more sense to get an outside agency to do the work. Using a reference librarian or university student to do some of the spadework need not be prohibitively expensive. Another argument for getting professional research is that it may carry more clout with investors.

Whatever the cost of the research, you need to assess its value to you when you are setting your budget. If getting it wrong would cost £100,000, £5000 spent on market research might be a good investment.

5. *Select the research technique(s):* If you cannot get the data you require from desk research, you will need to go out and find it yourself. Having to get the information yourself is good news rather than bad, as it means in all probability you will be the only person with the facts. The options for such research are described later in this chapter, under 'Field research'.

6. *Construct the research sample population:* It is rarely possible or even desirable to include every possible customer or competitor in your research. You therefore have to decide how big a sample you need to give you a reliable indication of how the whole population will behave.

7. *Process and analyse the data:* The raw market research data needs to be analysed and turned into information to guide your decisions on price, promotion and location, and on shape, design and scope of the product or service itself.

Enough is enough – constructing research populations

The size of the survey that you undertake is important. You frequently hear of political opinion polls taken on

Table 4.1 Survey size and accuracy

With a random sample of ...	95% of surveys are right within ... percentage points
250	6.2
500	4.4
750	3.6
1000	3.1
2000	2.2
6000	1.2

samples of 1500–2000 voters. This kind of information is important because the accuracy of your survey clearly increases with the size of the sample, as Table 4.1 shows:

So, if on a sample size of 600 your survey showed that 40 per cent of women in the town drove cars, the true proportion would probably lie between 36 and 44 per cent. For a new venture a minimum sample of 250 completed replies is usually acceptable.

Andrews University in the United States offers a free set of lecture notes explaining the subject of sample size comprehensively (www.andrews.edu). Auditnet (www.auditnet.org) provides some great Excel spreadsheets that do the boring maths of calculating sample size and accuracy for you. @ResearchInfo.com (www.researchinfo.com) gives the basics of writing a program for conducting your own questionnaire on the Internet.

How average is average?

The most common way information is considered is as a single figure that purports in some way to be representative of a population at large. Usually referred to as the average, this is the most often confused and frequently misrepresented number in any piece of business research. Knowing which average to use and when will impress investors enormously and go a long way to inspire confidence in the rest of the facts you are presenting.

To analyse any research you first need a 'data set' such as that in Table 4.2. This shows the range of prices being charged by the five competitors currently operating in a market we plan to enter, obtained from our study of the market.

Table 4.2 The selling prices of company products

Product	Selling price
A	30
B	40
C	10
D	15
E	10

The possible averages are as follows:

The mean: This is the most common kind of average and is used as a rough-and-ready check for many types of data. In the example above, adding up the prices (£105) and dividing by the number of suppliers (5), you arrive at a mean or average selling price of £21. However, if you decided to set your price in this area you would be significantly out of line with most of the other suppliers.

The median: This is the value occurring at the centre of a data set. Recasting the figures in Table 4.2 puts company D's selling price of £15 in that position, with two higher and two lower prices. The median comes into its own in situations where the outlying values in a data set are extreme, as they are in our example, where in fact most of the products sell for well below £21. In this case the median would be a better measure of the average. You should always use the median when the distribution is skewed. You can use either the mean or the median when the population is symmetrical, as they will give very similar results.

The mode: This is the observation in a data set that appears the most often; in this example it is £10. So although as we know the average price is £21 as expressed as a mean, it is highly likely based on the mode that most customers are only prepared to pay £10.

The range: As well as measuring how values cluster around a central value, to make full use of the data set we need to establish how much those values could vary. The range, calculated as the maximum figure minus the minimum figure, gives us an idea of how dispersed the data is and so how meaningful the mean figure alone might be. In the example being used here that is £40 − £10 = £30.

DESK RESEARCH

There is an increasing amount of data available in published form and accessible either online or via business sections of public libraries throughout the world to enable new business starters both to quantify the size of the market sectors they are entering and to determine trends in those markets. In addition to populations of cities and towns (helping to start the quanti-fication of markets), libraries frequently purchase Mintel Reports, which involve studies of growth in different business sectors. Government statistics, showing trends in the economy, are also held (*Annual Abstracts* for the economy as a whole, *Business Monitor* for individual sectors).

If you plan to sell to other companies or shops, *Kompass* and *Kelly's* directories list all company names and addresses (includ-ing buyers' telephone numbers). Many industrial sectors are represented by trade associations, which can provide informa-tion (see *Directory of British Associations*, published by CBD Research), while Chambers of Commerce are good sources of reference for import/export markets.

Here are some readily available sources of desk research data that an entrepreneur can use without tapping deeply into the budget:

- *Applegate* (www.applegate.co.uk) has information on 237,165 companies cross-referenced to 57,089 products in the UK and Ireland. It has a neat facility that allows you to search out the top businesses and people in any industry.
- *Business.com* (www.business.com) contains some 400,000 listings in 25,000 industry, product and service sub-categories. Useful for general industry background or details about a particular product line.
- *Chambers of Commerce* (www.chamberonline.co.uk) runs import/export clubs, offers international trade contacts and provides market research and online intelligence through a 150-country network of chambers. Its Link2Exports (www.link2exports.co.uk) website provides specific information on export markets by industry sector and country.
- *Companies House* (www.companieshouse.gov.uk) is the official repository of all company information in the UK. Its WebCHeck service offers a free Company Names and Address Index covering 2 million companies, searchable either by name or by unique company registration number. You can use WebCHeck to purchase a company's latest accounts, giving details of sales, profits, margins, directors, shareholders and bank borrowings, at a cost of £1 per company.
- *Corporate Information* (www.corporateinformation.com) is a business information site covering the main world economies, offering plenty of free information. It links to sources of business information in over 100 countries.
- *Easy Searcher 2* (www.easysearcher.com) is a collection of 400 search engines, both general and specialist, available on drop-down menus and listed by category.

- *Euro Info Centres* (www.euro-info.org.uk) is a network of 250 centres across Europe providing local access to a range of specialist information and advisory services to help business owners expand. Its services include advice on funding as well as help with market information through its network contacts and specialist information services.
- *Kelly's* (www.kellysearch.co.uk) lists information on 200,000 product and service categories across 200 countries. Business contact details, basic product and service details and online catalogues are provided.
- *Key Note* (www.keynote.co.uk) has built a reputation as an expert provider of market information, producing highly respected off-the-shelf publications that cover a comprehensive range of market sectors, from commercial and industrial to service and consumer titles. Reports are priced from around £300 upwards, with most in the £500–700 range.
- *Kompass* (www.kompass.com) claims to have details of 1.6 million UK companies, 23 million key product and service references, 3.2 million executive names, 744,000 trade and brand names and 50,000 Kompass classification codes in its UK directory. It also creates directory information in over 70 countries. Its website has a free area that users may access without registration.
- *Lexis-Nexis* (www.lexis-nexis.com) has literally dozens of databases covering every sector you can think of, but most useful for researching competitors is Company Analyzer, which creates comprehensive company reports drawn from 36 separate sources, with up to 250 documents per source providing access to accurate information about a company.
- *Mintel* (www.mintel.com) publishes over 400 reports every year examining every conceivable consumer market. Reports cost several hundred pounds, but you can view the introduction and main headings on the website. Most are available

free in business libraries. Mintel also offers a number of reports on US and European markets.

- *National Statistics* (www.statistics.gov.uk) contains a vast range of official UK statistics and information about those statistics, which can be accessed and downloaded free.
- *Online Newspapers* (www.onlinenewspapers.com) lists virtually every online newspaper in the world. Newspapers and magazines are a source of considerable information on companies, markets and products in the sphere of interest they cover. You can search straight from the homepage, either by continent or county. You can also find the 50 most popular online newspapers from a link at the top centre of the homepage. There is also a separate link for online magazines.
- *Research and Markets* (www.researchandmarkets.co.uk) is a one-stop shop that holds nearly 400,000 market research reports listed in 100 or so categories and across over 70 countries. Reports are priced from €20 upwards.
- *Thomas Global Register* (www.thomasglobal.com) is an online directory in 11 languages with details of over 700,000 suppliers in 28 countries. It can be searched by industry subsector or name, either for the world or by country.
- *World Market Research Associations* (www.mrweb.com), while not quite covering the world, does have web addresses for over 65 national market research associations and 100 or so other bodies, such as the Mystery Shopping Providers Association, which in turn has over 150 members worldwide.

USING THE INTERNET

The Internet is a rich source of market data, much of it free and immediately available. But you can't always be certain that the information is reliable or free of bias, as it can be difficult if not impossible to work out who exactly is providing it. That being said, you can get some valuable pointers as to whether or not what you plan to sell has a market, how big that market is and who else trades in that space. The following sources should be your starting points:

- *Google Trends* (www.google.co.uk/trends) provides a snapshot of what the world is most interested in at any one moment. For example, if you are thinking of starting a bookkeeping service, entering 'bookkeeping service' into the search pane produces a snazzy graph showing how interest measured by the number of searches is growing (or contracting) since January 2004 when Google started collecting the data. You can also see that South Africa has the greatest interest and the Netherlands the lowest. You can tweak the graph to show seasonality, thus demonstrating that Croydon registers the greatest interest in the UK overall and that demand peaks in September and bottoms out in November.
- *Google News* (www.google.com), which you can tap into by selecting 'News' on the horizontal menu at the top of the page under the Google banner, offers links to any newspaper article anywhere in the world covering a particular topic over the last decade or so, listed by year.
- *Microsoft* (http://adlab.microsoft.com) is testing a product that can give you a mass of data on market demographics (age, sex, income etc.), purchase intentions and a search funnel tool that helps you understand how your market searches the Internet. Using the demographics tool you can find that 76 per cent of people showing an interest in baby clothes are female, the peak age group is 25–34 year olds and the lowest-interest group is the under-18s, followed by the over-50s.

- *Inventory Overture* (http://inventory.overture.com/d/search-inventory/suggestion/) is a search tool showing how many people searched Yahoo! for a particular item. So for example, while 10,837 looked for either baby or baby and toddler clothing, only 927 searched for organic baby clothing, 167 for used baby clothing and 141 for cheap baby clothing: facts that give useful pointers as to the likely price sensitivity in this market.

- *Blogs* are sites where people, both informed and ignorant, converse about a particular topic. The information on blogs is more straw in the wind than fact. Globe of Blogs (www.globeofblogs.com), launched in 2002, claims to be the first comprehensive world weblog directory, with links to over 58,000 blogs, searchable by country, topic and almost any other criterion you care to name. Google (http://blogsearch.google.com) also offers a search engine to the world's blogs.

- *Trade Association Forum* (www.taforum.org) is a directory of trade associations, on whose websites are links to industry-relevant online research sources. For example, you will find the Baby Products Association listed, at whose website you can find details of the 238 companies operating in the sector, with their contact details.

- *Internet Public Library* (www.ipl.org) is run by a consortium of American universities, whose aim is to provide Internet users with help finding information online. There are extensive sections on business, computers, education, leisure and health.

- *Find Articles* (www.findarticles.com) aims to provide credible, freely available information you can trust. It has over 10 million articles from thousands of resources, with an archived dating back to 1984. You can see a summary of all articles and most are free, though in some cases you may need to pay a modest subscription, rarely more than a few pounds. You can restrict your search to those articles that are free by selecting 'free articles only' from the right-hand pull-down menu.

GETTING OUT THERE – THE IMPORTANCE OF FIELD RESEARCH

Most business research fieldwork carried out consists of interviews, with the interviewer putting questions to a respondent. The more popular forms of interview are currently personal (face-to-face) interview: 45 per cent (especially for consumer markets); telephone, e-mail and Web surveys: 42 per cent (especially for surveying companies); post 6 per cent (especially for industrial markets); and test and discussion groups: 7 per cent.

Personal interviews, Web surveys and postal surveys are clearly less expensive than getting together panels of interested parties or using expensive telephone time. Telephone interviewing requires a very positive attitude, courtesy, an ability not to talk too quickly and listening while sticking to a rigid questionnaire. Low response rates on postal surveys (less than 5 per cent is normal) can be improved by accompanying letters explaining the questionnaire's purpose and why respondents should reply, by offering rewards for completed questionnaires (small gifts), by sending reminder letters and, of course, by providing prepaid reply envelopes. Personally addressed e-mail questionnaires have secured higher response rates – as high as 10–15 per cent – as recipients have a greater tendency to read and respond to e-mail received in their private e-mail boxes. However, unsolicited e-mails ('spam') can cause vehement reactions. The key to success is the same as with postal surveys – the mailing should feature an explanatory letter and incentives for the recipient to open the questionnaire.

There are some basic rules for good questionnaire design, however the questions are to be administered:

1. Keep the number of questions to a minimum.
2. Keep the questions simple! Answers should be either 'Yes/No/Don't know' or at least four alternatives.
3. Avoid ambiguity – make sure that the respondent really understands the question (avoid 'generally', 'usually', 'regularly').
4. Seek factual answers and avoid opinions.
5. Make sure that at the beginning you have a cut-out question to eliminate unsuitable respondents (e.g. those who never use the product/service).
6. At the end, make sure that you have an identifying question to show the cross-section of respondents.

Having a suitable sample size is vital if reliance is to be placed on survey data. How to calculate the appropriate sample size is explained above.

TESTING THE MARKET

The ultimate form of market research is to find some real customers to buy and use your product or service before you spend too much time and money on it. The ideal way to do this is to sell into a limited area or small section of your market. In that way, if things don't quite work out as you expect you won't have upset too many people.

This may involve buying in a small quantity of product, as you need to fulfil orders in order to test your ideas fully. Once you have found a small number of people who are happy with your product, price and delivery/execution and have paid up, you can proceed with a little more confidence than if all your ideas are just on paper.

Bagel Express – piloting a US idea in the UK

David Sinclair started his fast-food bagel company 'when he was 24. His idea was sparked during an overseas trip: 'When I was backpacking my way round America on Greyhound buses, at one station in Vermont I saw a huge queue at what turned out to be a bagel stand. I'd hardly ever heard of bagels even though they were sold all over the States.' When he returned home he discovered that bagels were then only sold as fast food in a handful of outlets: 'They were very much a Jewish secret,' he said. He piloted the idea by taking a small stall at Liverpool railway station for three months and within two years he had opened eight bagel shops.

Unless you research the market you run a real risk that your 'hunch' will prove to be little more than a blind alley. Research is vital preparation that will enable you to launch a business confidently and attract investors. However, it's not the only foundation work you need to do. Your investors will also want to see a credible business plan.

Chapter 5

Mastering the 'master plan' – business plans are templates, not straitjackets

Imagine you are setting off for a well-deserved break. You drop your car off at the airport, pile the bags onto a trolley and stroll into the departure lounge. Selecting a queue that seems to be moving, you work your way forward to the check-in desk. At that point you hit your first snag. While you may have had a general idea that a destination with sun and a beach is what you have in mind, that's as far as your plans have been formulated. Without a passport, ticket, hotel reservation or foreign currency, the airport lounge is about as far as you are likely to get. In fact, you may not even get this far without taking some important decisions in advance: where you are going, for how long, where you will be staying and how you will foot the bill.

By now I guess you are thinking that this scenario is too unrealistic to be worth considering. No sane person would embark on anything as expensive or as important to their personal well-being as a holiday without having done some thorough research and preparation, would they? The better organised among us would have a file with all the relevant documents, a budget for costs, travel insurance and arrangements for security at home in our absence. True, this would all have taken time, but it would have provided the peace of mind that is so essential to get the best out of a holiday. For some of us the planning itself would have been part of the enjoyment.

So for something really important, even life changing such as starting a business that we hope will make us seriously rich, surely everyone will have a plan? According to research carried out at Cranfield School of Management, many of the fastest-growing and most successful businesses started out with a written business plan. If many businesses begin without a business plan, you could be forgiven for thinking that preparing one is a luxury you can live without. Time is short and it is surely more important to find some customers and get selling. Beguiling though this may sound, the statistics are against you. Ventures started without a written business plan are nearly twice as likely to fail as those that have one. Research from Cranfield also demonstrates clearly that globally, owner-managed firms with business plans outperform those without, both in terms of sales and profits, those key determinants of future value. The truth is that if you're going to get the support you need, fulfil your growth potential and ultimately sell the business for millions of pounds, a business plan is well nigh essential.

Boden – without a plan and losing money

Johnnie Boden's first catalogue was hand-drawn by a friend with just eight items. That was back in 1991 and since then the business has come from bedroom to boardroom by way of a near catastrophic lack of capital. The mail-order clothes company now competes with Gap, Marks & Spencer and John Lewis for a slice of the mainstream fashion market, with sales of £129.5 million, profits of £22.75 million and over 600 employees dispatching over 3000 orders every day from its warehouse.

Boden (www.boden.co.uk) has reason to feel pleased. But it very nearly wasn't the success story it undoubtedly is. In an interview with *Real Business* (www.realbusiness.co.uk), Johnnie Boden explained why for the first three years the company was losing money hand over fist. 'We kept on running out of cash,' he said. 'Although the concept was strong, I had no decent business plan.'

SO WHY DON'T ENTREPRENEURS PLAN?

Preparing a comprehensive business plan takes time and effort, but costs little. In our experience gleaned from Cranfield's new enterprise programmes, anything between 100 and 200 man-hours is needed, depending on the nature of your business and how much data you have already gathered. Despite the obvious benefits, thousands of would-be entrepreneurs still attempt to start without a business plan. The most common among these are businesses that either appear to need little or no capital at the outset or whose founders have funds of their own. In both these cases it is believed to be unnecessary to expose the project to harsh financial appraisal.

The former hypothesis is usually based on the easily exploded myth that customers will all pay cash on the nail and suppliers will wait for months to be paid. In the meantime, the proprietor has the use of these funds to finance the business. Such model customers and suppliers are thinner on the ground than optimistic entrepreneurs think. In any event, two important market rules still apply: either the product or service on offer fails to sell like hot cakes and mountains of unpaid stock build up, all of which eventually have to be financed; or it does sell like hot cakes and more financially robust entrepreneurs are attracted into the market. Without the staying power that adequate financing provides, these new competitors will rapidly kill the initial business off.

MANY ENTREPRENEURS PREFER ACTION TO WORDS – BUT YOU REALLY NEED BOTH

Those would-be entrepreneurs with funds of their own, or worse still borrowed from 'innocent' friends and relatives, tend to think that the time spent in preparing a business plan could be more usefully (and enjoyably) spent looking for premises, buying a new car or installing a computer. In short, anything that inhibits them from immediate action is viewed as wasting time. As most people's perception of their business venture is flawed in some important respect, it follows that jumping in at the deep end is risky – and unnecessarily so. Flaws can often be discovered cheaply and in advance when preparing a business plan; they are always discovered in the marketplace, invariably at a much higher and usually fatal cost.

There was a myth at the start of the Internet boom that the pace of development in that sector was too fast for business planning. The first generation of dot-com businesses and their backers seemed happy to pump money into what they called a 'business' or 'revenue' model. These 'models' were brief statements of intent supported by little more than wishful thinking. Soon those pioneers were swept into a historical junkyard leaving behind only those such as Amazon (see the case example in Chapter 1) with better plans and deeper pockets.

A great business needs equally great resources. These include investors and lenders of course, prospective partners certainly and employees probably. All these are audiences that will hang on to every word in your business plan. They are not unreasonably trying to gauge just how your business will help them to achieve their own goals and what the risks and rewards are for them. In a nutshell: no business plan, no hope of pulling in the money or talent needed to unlock a super venture's real potential.

The first thing you will discover about a business plan is that things never work out the way you hope or expect. Customers change their minds, suppliers deliver late, new competitors appear out of the blue and staff disappoint or disappear. As Helmuth von Moltke, chief of staff of the Prussian Army, succinctly expressed it: 'no battle plan survives contact with the enemy'. But that didn't mean he didn't believe in planning; quite the opposite. He believed that sound military strategy meant that military leaders had to prepare extensively for all possible outcomes.

Every business can have a less rocky start than Boden if it begins with a soundly based business plan rather than ending up with one to rescue it from the brink of catastrophe. While preparing a plan can take a couple of week's hard work, that can be spread over the months before you commit to the venture. There are at least four compelling reasons why every business founder should start out with a business plan.

1. *It gives you confidence in the concept:* Carrying out the basic customer and competitor research that is the foundation of any business plan gives you a greater certainty that the business will actually work. All businesses have a number of wrinkles that can be smoothed out when preparing the business plan, at a much lower cost than by letting your customers tell you later.

2. *It clarifies the scale of resources needed:* Although in the founder's own words Boden was not a 'swanky start-up', he did pump in £300,000 early on. With hindsight, he felt that the company really needed double that sum to have a decent chance of success, but as Boden started with money from a legacy left by an uncle, he not unnaturally wanted to live within those means.

3. *It improves your financing prospects:* Since Johnnie Boden inherited a legacy he was able to sidestep some of the problems of raising money. But most start-ups need some money, even if it is only by way of a bank loan or overdraft. And the more successful you are, the more money you need. Typically a mail-order business has £1 of capital invested to generate £2 of sales, so while Boden could squeak by with £300,000 when its turnover was less than £2 million, now it needs more like £50 million.

4. *It rehearses you for the future:* Your business plan should assume success and set out the resources needed to scale up quickly as soon as that success is realised. Other entrepreneurs are always on the look-out for opportunities and if you leave them an opening they will not be slow in carving out a niche for themselves. When your business hits its ambitious targets, grows and takes on staff, you will have a basis from which to prepare and update business plans on a regular basis. This will be one of the primary ways of involving everyone in your business in shaping future plans and putting them into effect. No one expects every event recorded on a business plan to occur as predicted, but the understanding and knowledge created by the process of business planning will prepare the business for any changes it may face, and so enable you to adjust quickly.

Preparing a business plan is therefore essential if you are both to crystallise and focus your ideas, and test your resolve about entering or expanding your business. Once completed, your business plan will serve as a blueprint to follow that, like any map, improves the user's chances of reaching the destination.

WHAT GOES INTO THE PLAN?

While there is no such thing as a 'universal' business plan format, certain layouts and contents seem to have gone down better than others. These are some guidelines for producing an attractive business plan, from both an owner's and a financier's perspective:

- *Cover and table of contents:* First, the cover should show the name of the business, the date on which the plan was prepared and your name, addresses (including e-mail), phone number and mobile number. Anyone reading the business plan may want to talk over some aspects of the proposal before arranging a meeting. Having written the business plan you will know exactly where everything in it is, but any other reader needs some pointers to guide them through the maze: that's what the table of contents does. Number each main section – marketing, finance, people and so forth – 1, 2, 3; important elements within a section can then be designated 1.1, 1.2 and so on.
- *Executive summary:* This is the most important part of your plan and will form the heart of your 'elevator pitch' (see below). Written last, the summary should be punchy, short – ideally one page but never more than two – and enthuse any reader. Its primary purpose is to get an outsider, bank manager, business angel or prospective partner to want to read the rest of the business plan.
- *Marketing:* Information on the product/service on offer, customers and the size of the market, competitors, proposed pricing, promotion and selling methods.

- **Operations:** Information on any processes such as manufacture, assembly, purchasing, stock holding, delivery/fulfilment and website.
- **Financial projections:** Information on sales and cash flow for the next 12–18 months, showing how much money is needed, for what and by when. As well as cash flow, these projections should show when you will break even and the scope of the profit opportunity.
- **Risk assessment:** This features high on your readers' list of concerns, so you should anticipate as many as you can, together with your solution. For example: 'Our strategy is highly dependent on finding a warehouse with a cold store for stock. But if we can't find one by start date we will use space in the public cold store 10 miles away. This is not as convenient but it will do.'
- **Exit strategy:** Detail an exit route for venture capitalists and business angels. Investors, yourself included, are in it for the money. They don't just want to see how you can make a profit, that's a given for any super venture. They want to see how value is going to be crystallised into serious wealth. You need to able to point out hungry big players in your market with a proven appetite for acquisitions; or to a track record of stock market floats for comparable businesses to your own. Typically, they are looking to liquidate their investments within three to seven years, so your business plan should not only show them how much money they can make but when and how they can get their investment out.
- **Premises:** The space and equipment that will be needed.
- **People:** The skills and experience you have that will help you run this business; what other people you need and where you will find them.
- **Administrative matters:** Whether you have any IP (intellectual property) on your product or service; what insurance you need; what bookkeeping and accounting system you plan

to use; how you will keep customer, supplier and employee records.

- *Milestone timetable:* This should show the key actions you still have to take to be ready to sell your product or service and the dates by which these will be completed.
- *Appendices:* Use these for any bulky information such as market studies, competitors' leaflets, customer endorsements, technical data, patents, CVs and the like that you refer to in your business plan.

The break-even analysis

This is a technique that requires you to grasp that there are fundamentally two different types of cost. Fixed costs are those that don't vary with the volume of output. So the rent on, say, a retail outlet remains 'fixed' irrespective of the amount of sales actually achieved. That doesn't of course mean that the cost itself is fixed, as the landlord could change the rent. Variable costs are those that do change with sales levels. So a retailer would need to buy in stock to meet rising demand and a manufacturer will need more raw materials and more workers' hours.

The break-even equation is:

$$\text{Break-even point} = \frac{\text{Fixed costs}}{\text{Selling price} - \text{Unit variable cost}}$$

So if the rent is £10,000 (fixed costs), the selling price is £5 and the cost of buying in the only product you sell is £3, then the break-even point is 5000 units. If your goal is to make £10,000 profit, by adding that amount to the fixed costs you can see that sales then need to reach 10,000 units.

There are a number of online spreadsheets and tutorials that will take you through the process of calculating the break-even point. For example, biz/ed (www.bized.co.uk) has a Virtual Learning Arcade section that includes a simulation letting you see the effect of changing variables on a fairly complex break-even calculation. Score (www.score.org>Business Tools>Template Gallery>Break Even Analysis) and BizPep (www.bizpeponline.com) sell a software program that calculates your break-even for prices plus or minus 50 per cent of your proposed selling price. You can tweak costs to see how to optimise your selling price and so hit your profit goal.

Cash and profits – what's the difference?

There is a saying in business that profit is vanity and cash flow is sanity. Both are necessary but in the short term, often that is all that matters. To a new business as it struggles to get a foothold in the shifting sands of trading, cash flow is life or death.

Cash is not that difficult to understand: it is any funds in the bank, in your hand or available to you from a bank by way of an overdraft. Your cash-flow projection sets out to assess the timing of cash in and out of the business, allowing for such factors as how long it will take customers to pay up and when you in turn have to pay suppliers.

Profit, unlike cash, is less a matter of fact and more a matter of opinion. Take a situation where a business buys in products for resale for £1 million, planning to mark them up by 100 per cent and sell them for £2 million. To get such a great margin, it has to buy and pay for everything in advance. At the end of the first three months, stock costing £25,000 has been sold, netting £500,000. So the business has not yet reached cash-flow break-even, but is it profitable? The matching principle, an accounting rule that says we should match income and expenditure to the relevant time period, comes into play here. So yes, the business has made a paper profit of £25,000 (£50,000 – £25,000) in the first three months of trading. But it is still operating at £500,000 negative on its cash flow, money it must have raised from somewhere and is still liable for. It is sitting on an asset, stock, which cost £75,000 and is yet to be sold. But suppose the product in question is superseded or a competitor comes in at a much lower price; the value of that stock could be reduced or even eliminated. So in the worst case where the stock is worthless, the business would have paid out £1 million and received back only £500,000 in sales – making a loss of £500,000. Thus it is quite possible for a business that is very profitable in one period to be completely worthless in a matter of months or even days.

If you think this an unlikely scenario, look back to Lehman Brothers, the 158-year-old bank that failed in September 2008. It was listed 37th in the Fortune 500 in 2008, up from 47th the preceding year. Its last accounts showed $4192 million profits, up 4.6 per cent on the year before. Its 'stock in trade' was investment advice, which became worthless as its business model imploded.

MAKING YOUR BUSINESS PLAN STAND OUT

Let's not mince words. Most business plans are dull, badly written and frequently read only by the most junior of people in the financing organisations they're presented to. One venture capital firm in the United States went on record to say that in one year it received 25,000 business plans asking for finance and invested in only 40.

Follow these tips to make your business plan stand out from the crowd:

- *Hit them with the benefits:* You need to spell out exactly what you do, for whom and why that matters. One such statement that has the ring of practical authority is: 'Our website makes ordering gardening products simple. It saves the average customer two hours a week browsing catalogues and £250 a year through discounts not otherwise available from garden centres. We have surveyed 200 home gardeners, who rate efficient purchasing as a key priority.'
- *Make your projections believable:* Sales projections always look like a hockey stick and a straight line curving rapidly upwards towards the end. You have to explain exactly what drives growth, how you capture sales and what the link between activity and results is. The profit margins are key numbers in your projections, alongside sales forecasts. Financiers tend to probe these figures in depth, so show the build-up in detail.
- *Say how big the market is:* Financiers feel safer backing people in big markets. Capturing a fraction of a percentage of a massive market may be hard to achieve, but if you get it at least the effort is worth it. Going for 10 per cent of a market measured in millions rather than billions may come to the same number, but the result isn't as interesting.
- *Introduce yourself and your team:* Investors hate one-man bands, so you a need a team to launch a big business, preferably one who sound like winners with a track record of great accomplishments. If possible include non-executive directors; sometimes a heavyweight outsider can lend extra credibility to a business proposition. If you know or have access to

someone with a successful track record in your area of business who has time on their hands, you can invite them to help. Non-executive directors do need to have relevant experience or be able to open doors and do deals. Check out organisations such as Venture Investment Partners (www.ventureip.co.uk) and the Independent Director Initiative (www.independentdirector.co.uk), a joint venture between Ernst & Young and the Institute of Directors, for information on tracking down the right non-executive director for your business.

- *Provide financial forecasts:* You need projected cash flows, profit and loss accounts and balance sheets for at least three years ahead. No one believes them after Year 1, but the thinking behind them is what's important.
- *Demonstrate the product or service:* Financiers need to see what the customer is going to get. A mock-up is okay or, failing that, a picture or diagram. For a service, show how customers can gain from using it and that it can help with improved production scheduling and so reduce stock holding, for example.
- *Spell out the benefits to your potential investors:* Tell them that you can pay their money within x years, even on your most cautious projections. Or if you are speaking to an equity investor, tell them what return they may get on their investment when you sell the business in three or five years' time.

TIPS ON COMMUNICATING THE PLAN

You are going to show your business plan to some very experienced people in order to get the backing that any venture with serious prospects of success must do, so you need to take some steps to ensure that the way it is put together reflects the work that has been carried out and the value of your proposition. Only if you are seen to take your business plan seriously can you expect others to do the same, so think about the following:

- *Packaging:* Appropriate packaging enhances every product and a business plan is no exception. A simple spiral binding with a plastic cover on the front and back makes it easy for the reader to move from section to section, and it ensures that the plan will survive frequent handling.
- *Writing clearly:* You and any partners should write the first draft of the business plan yourselves. The niceties of grammar and style can be resolved later. When your first draft has been revised, then comes the task of editing. Here the grammar, spelling and language must be carefully checked to ensure that your business plan is crisp, correct, clear and complete – and not too long; 10–15 pages will be more than sufficient in most cases.

A 'prospectus', such as a business plan seeking finance from investors, can have legal status, turning any claims you may make for sales and profits (for example) into a 'contract'. Your accountant and legal adviser will be able to help you with the appropriate language that can convey your projections without giving them contractual status.

This would also be a good time to talk over the proposal with a friendly financier, not necessarily one you are approaching for money. They can give an insider's view on the strengths and weaknesses of your proposal. These people see thousands of proposals each year and there is much to be discovered, especially from the ones they don't back.

PRESENTATION TECHNIQUES

If getting someone interested in your business plan is half the battle in raising funds, the other half is the oral presentation.

Any organisation financing a venture will insist on seeing the person or team involved presenting and defending their plans. They know that they are backing the people every bit as much as the idea. You can be sure that any financier you are presenting to will be well prepared.

These are the points to bear in mind when preparing for the presentation of your business plan:

- Find out how much time you have, then rehearse your presentation beforehand. Allow at least as much time for questions as for your talk.
- Use visual aids and if possible bring and demonstrate your product or service. A video or computer-generated model is better than nothing.
- Explain your strategy in a businesslike manner, demonstrating your grasp of the competitive market forces at work. Listen to comments and criticisms carefully, avoiding a defensive attitude when you respond.
- Make your replies to questions brief and to the point. If potential investors want more information, they can ask. This approach allows time for the many different questions that must be asked, either now or later, before an investment can proceed.
- Your goal is to create empathy between yourself and your listener(s). While you may not be able to change your personality, you could take a few tips on presentation skills. Eye contact, tone of speech, enthusiasm and body language all have a part to play in making a presentation successful.
- Wearing a suit is never likely to upset anyone. Shorts and sandals could just set the wrong tone! Serious money calls for serious people.
- Be prepared. You need to have every aspect of your business plan in your head and know your way around the plan forwards, backwards and sideways. You never know when

the chance to present may occur. It's as well to have 5-, 10- and 20-minute presentations ready to run at a moment's notice.

THE ELEVATOR PITCH – WHEN EVERY WORD COUNTS

Often the person you are pitching your proposal to is short of time. As a rough rule of thumb, the closer you get to an individual with the power to make decisions, the less time you will get to make your pitch. So you need to have a short presentation to hand that can be made in any circumstance – in a plane, at an airport or between floors in a lift – hence the name 'elevator pitch'.

Pacific Direct – a successful elevator pitch

Lara Morgan, founder of hotel toiletries supplier Pacific Direct, had come a long way from the garage in Bedford, England, where she started up her business, when she had the opportunity to pitch for a strategic alliance with one of the most influential players in her market. The scene was set for her to make a relaxed pitch over coffee at the Dorchester Hotel in Park Lane, London, when at a moment's notice the situation changed dramatically. Lara was told that due to a diary change she had 15 minutes in a chauffeur-driven limousine en route to Harrods to make her proposition.

She was prepared, she made her presentation and she secured a deal that was instrumental in creating Pacific's unique 5-star hotel strategy. Pacific now has Penhaligon's, Elemis, Ermenegildo Zegna, Nina

Campbell, Floris, The White Company and Natural Products in its world-class product portfolio. Lara sold her business in 2008 to private equity house Primary Capital for £20 million.

USING A NON-DISCLOSURE AGREEMENT (NDA) – KEEPING YOUR IDEA SAFE

Finding an investor or a bank to lend to your business may take weeks or months. During that time, potential investors diligently gather information about the business so that they don't have surprises later about income, expenses or undisclosed liabilities. The business plan is only the starting point for their investigations.

If you and the prospective financiers are strangers to one another, you may be reluctant to turn over sensitive business information until you are confident that they are serious. (This is not as sensitive an issue with banks as it is with business angels and venture capital providers.) To allay these fears, consider asking for a confidentiality letter or agreement.

A confidentiality letter suffices in most circumstances. But if substantial amounts of intellectual property are involved, you may prefer to have a lawyer draft a longer, more formal confidentiality agreement, also known as a non-disclosure agreement (NDA). That's okay, but you (and perhaps your lawyer as well) should make sure that the proposed document contains no binding commitment on you. The confidentiality letter should be limited to the other party's agreement to treat the information as strictly confidential, to use the information only to investigate lending or investing in the business and to the other terms set out in the letter.

BUSINESS PLANNING SOFTWARE

There are a number of free software packages that will help you through the process of writing your business plan. The ones listed here include some useful resources, spreadsheets and tips that may speed up the process, but they are not substitutes for finding out the basic facts about your market, customers and competitors:

BizPlanIt (www.bizplanit.com) has free resources including free business plan information, advice, articles, links and resources, a free monthly newsletter and a Virtual Business Plan to pinpoint information.

Bplans.com (www.bplans.com), created by Palo Alto Software, offers thousands of pages of free sample plans, planning tools and expert advice to help you start and run your business. The site contains 60 free sample business plans and the software package, Business Plan Pro, has these plans plus a further 140. The sample business plans are tailored for every type of business, from aircraft rental to wedding gowns.

Royal Bank of Canada (www.royalbank.com) has a wide range of useful help for entrepreneurs as well as a business plan writer package and three sample business plans.

Whether you use software packages like these or simply construct the document from first principles, formulating a comprehensive business plan will not only focus your mind on the opportunities and risks that lie ahead, it will also assure potential backers that you have done some serious research and strategic thinking. A well-constructed plan will therefore make the process of finding investment a lot easier.

Chapter 6

The money – who has it and why you might just get your hands on some of it

Every venture that is of any substance will need capital invested in it. You might find that surprising, but the truth is that businesses that don't have money behind them are almost always without sufficient prospects to make anyone rich. Even if by some quirk of luck they have prospects of success and the market is large, without money it will be difficult to exploit the opportunity with sufficient speed to deter competitors from entering the market or to raise barriers to entry by branding or gaining intellectual property rights. Even dot-com service providers such as Money Supermarket, a case we looked at in Chapter 1, and Lastminute.com needed large dollops of cash to start up or grow. The moral is, if you want to get rich, you need to think about where you will find capital – and it's an issue that you need to address from the outset.

EVERY SUCCESSFUL BUSINESS NEEDS OUTSIDE MONEY SOMETIME

Go back 100 years or so and it had already become apparent that business ventures needed more money than an individual could readily raise on their own; or in the event of failure comfortably lose. The pool of business founders happy to risk everything from their home to a last shirt button was limited, to say the least. So to encourage entrepreneurs to take bold risks, a number of legal structures were developed to facilitate sharing that risk in a more equitable manner. The generic name for this risk capital is equity. The distinction between equity and any other type of funding is that those putting it up share risks and rewards together.

In the next chapter we will look at debt capital, usually provided by banks. They, theoretically, don't want to take any risk and don't expect to share the rewards. However, the events of 2008 left us with a rather different view of banks and the risks they are prepared to take.

Cobra Beer – raising cash to fund growth

In 1990, Cambridge-educated and recently qualified accountant Karan Bilimoria started importing and distributing Cobra beer, a name he chose because it appeared to work well in lots of different languages. He initially supplied his beer to complement Indian restaurant food in the UK. Lord Bilimoria, as he now is, started out with debts of £20,000, but from a small flat in Fulham and with just a Citroën CV by way of assets, he has grown his business to sales of over £100 million a year.

> Three factors have been key to its success. Cobra was originally sold in large 660ml bottles and so was more likely to be shared by diners. Also Cobra is less fizzy than European lagers, so drinkers are less likely to feel bloated and can eat and drink more. The third factor was Bilimoria's extensive knowledge through his training as an accountant of sources of finance for a growing business. He was fortunate in having an old-style bank manager who had such belief in Cobra that he agreed a loan of £30,000, but since then he has tapped into every possible type of funding, including selling a 28 per cent stake in his firm in 1995.

WHAT DO INVESTORS WANT?

The fundamental question is, of course, what are investors looking for? Unsurprisingly, they are using something like the magic formula outlined in Chapter 1, which I recommend you use to evaluate a business opportunity for yourself. Investors would like the problem your product or service addresses to be a big one; they would like to see that your solution is scalable and that there is some discernible barrier preventing others from entering your market too quickly. They do want a few other things as well, including some evidence of customer acceptance. Put simply, backers like to know that your new product or service will sell and is being used, even if only on a trial or demonstration basis. For instance, the founder of Solicitec, a company selling software to solicitors to enable them to process relatively standard documents such as wills, had little trouble in getting support for his house-conveyancing package once his product had been tried and approved by a leading building society for its panel of solicitors.

However, if you are only at the prototype stage, then as well as having to assess your chances of succeeding with technology, financiers have no immediate indication that, once made, your product will appeal to the market. Under these circumstances, you have to show not only that the 'problem' your innovation seeks to solve is substantial, but that it is one that a large number of people will have a compelling need to pay for within a foreseeable timescale. For instance, one inventor from the Royal College of Art came up with a revolutionary toilet system design that, as well as being extremely thin, used 30 per cent less water per flush and had half the number of moving parts of a conventional product, all for no increase in price. Although he had only drawings to show potential investors, it was clear that with domestic metred water for all households a distinct possibility and a UK market of half a million new units per annum, a sizeable degree of acceptance was reasonably certain.

As well as evidence of customer acceptance, entrepreneurs need to demonstrate that they know how and to whom their new product or service must be sold, and that they have a financially viable means of doing so.

They also need the right personal qualities. At the end of the day, every investment boils down to people. So you, your career progression, your knowledge, skills and experience will all be uppermost in an investor's mind when reviewing your proposition. For example Tim Waterstone, whose case we looked at in Chapter 1, had first-hand experience of running a chain of bookshops.

Investors, as we have already noted, are rarely interested in supporting one-man bands. They want the security of having a team, even if it's only a team of two. They also know that few people have all the skills needed to get a substantial venture off the ground. Blooming Marvellous, Bebo and Money Supermarket are examples where the different skill sets that teams can bring beyond that of a single entrepreneur formed an important factor. Investors also know that teamwork is essential if the business is to become valuable and the sooner they see that attribute being exhibited the better.

The presence of a team implies that the business is a legal entity rather than merely an individual with a good idea. Investors will look carefully at the legal status of that entity.

SOLE TRADERS AND PARTNERSHIPS

Being a sole trader is the simplest form of legal structure for a business enterprise. It has two fundamental weaknesses that make it unsuited to creating serious wealth: the only money that a sole trader can raise is debt and that carries risk; and there is no distinction in law or taxation between a sole trader's business and his or her personal assets.

Partnerships are effectively collections of sole traders and, as such, share the legal problems attached to personal liability. There are very few restrictions to setting up in business with another person (or persons) in partnership, and several definite advantages. By pooling resources you may have more capital; you will be bringing, hopefully, several sets of skills to the business; and if one of you is ill the business can still carry on.

Partner pitfalls

There are two serious drawbacks to a partnership that you should certainly consider. First, if your partner makes a business mistake, perhaps by signing a disastrous contract, without your knowledge or consent, every member of the partnership must shoulder the consequences. Under these circumstances your personal assets could be taken to pay the creditors, even though the mistake was no fault of your own.

Second, if your partner goes bankrupt in his or her personal capacity, for whatever reason, his or her share of the partnership can be seized by creditors. As a private individual you are not liable for your partner's private debts, but having to buy him or her out of the partnership at short notice could put you and the business in financial jeopardy. Even death may not release you from partnership obligations and in some circumstances your estate can remain liable. Unless you take 'public' leave of your partnership by notifying your business contacts and legally bringing your partnership to an end, you could remain liable.

Partnerships – the legal lowdown

The legal regulations governing this field are set out in the Partnership Act 1890, which in essence assumes that competent businesspeople should know what they are doing. The Act merely provides a framework of agreement that applies 'in the absence of agreement to the contrary'. It follows from this that many partnerships are entered into without legal formalities – and sometimes without the parties themselves being aware that they have entered a partnership!

The main provisions of the Partnership Act state:

- All partners contribute capital equally.
- All partners share profits and losses equally.
- No partner shall have interest paid on his capital.
- No partner shall be paid a salary.
- All partners have an equal say in the management of the business.

Unless you are a member of certain professions (such as law and accountancy), you are restricted to a maximum of 20 partners in any partnership. It is unlikely that all of these provisions will suit you, so you would be well advised to get a partnership agreement drawn up in writing by a solicitor at the outset of your venture.

LIMITED PARTNERSHIPS

One possibility that can reduce the more painful consequences of entering a partnership is to form a limited partnership, combining the best attributes of a partnership and a company. A limited partnership works like this. There must be one or more general partners with the same basic rights and responsibilities (including unlimited liability) as in any general partnership, and one or more limited partners who are usually passive investors. The big difference between a general partner and a limited partner is that the limited partner isn't personally liable for debts of the partnership. The most a limited partner can lose is the amount that he or she:

- Paid or agreed to pay into the partnership as a capital contribution.
- Received from the partnership after it became insolvent.

To keep this limited liability, a limited partner may not participate in the management of the business, with very few exceptions. A limited partner who does get actively involved in the management of the business risks losing immunity from personal liability and having the same legal exposure as a general partner.

The advantage of a limited partnership as a business structure is that it provides a way for business owners to raise money (from the limited partners) without having either to take in new partners who will be active in the business, or to form a limited company. A general partnership that has been operating for years can also create a limited partnership to finance expansion.

LIMITED COMPANIES

The concept of limited liability, where the shareholders are not liable, in the last resort, for the debts of their business, changed the whole nature of business and risk taking. It opened the floodgates, encouraging a new generation of entrepreneurs to undertake much larger-scale ventures without taking on themselves all the consequences of failure. As the name suggests, in this form of business liability is limited to the amount you contribute by way of share capital and in the event of failure, creditors' claims are restricted to the assets of the company.

The concept of limited liability can be traced back to Roman times when it was granted, albeit infrequently, by those in power as a special favour to friends for large undertakings. The idea was resurrected in 1811 when New York State brought in a general limited liability law for manufacturing companies. Most American states followed suit and eventually Britain caught up in 1854. Today most countries have a legal structure incorporating the concept of limited liability.

Around half of all businesses are limited companies. A limited company, unlike a sole trader, has a legal identity of its own, separate from the people who own or run it. This means that, in the event of failure, creditors' claims are restricted to the assets of the company. The shareholders of the business are not liable as individuals for the business debts beyond the paid-up value of their shares. This applies even if the shareholders are working directors, unless of course the company has been trading fraudulently. The primary benefit is the freedom to raise capital by selling shares.

Disadvantages include the costs involved in setting up the company and the legal requirement in some cases for the company's accounts to be audited by a chartered or certified accountant. Usually it is only businesses with assets approaching £3 million that have to be audited but if, for example, you have shareholders who own more than 10 per cent of your firm they can ask for the accounts to be audited.

The behaviour of companies and their directors is governed by the company law of the country in which they operate and sometimes that law has a very long arm. For example, there are directors of UK enterprises either in US gaols or in the process of being extradited for offences that were not crimes in the UK when the activities in question were committed.

Directors and their duties

You as the business founder will be a director of the limited company. As such, you will have to cope with some technical, more detailed requirements, for example sending in the accounts to the regulatory authorities, appointing an auditor if required, holding regular board meetings and keeping shareholders informed. More onerous than merely signing the accounts, a director is expected and required in law to understand the significance of the balance sheet, profit and loss account and cashflow statement.

A director's duties, responsibilities and potential liabilities include:

1. To act in good faith in the interests of the company. This includes carrying out duties diligently and honestly.

2. Not to carry on the business of the company with intent to defraud creditors or for any fraudulent purpose.
3. Not knowingly to allow the company to trade while insolvent ('wrongful trading'). Directors who do so may have to pay for the debts incurred by the company while insolvent.
4. Not to deceive shareholders.
5. To have a regard for the interests of the employees in general.
6. To comply with the requirements of the Companies Acts, such as providing what is needed in terms of accounting records or filing accounts.

Limited liability is a privilege, not a right

The sting in the tail is that limited liability is a privilege, not a right, and as such can be withdrawn. There are three types of activities that directors need to steer clear of if they don't want to be disqualified, jailed or made personally liable for the debts and liabilities of any company in which they are involved. Disqualification means that not only can you not run a company, but if you issued your orders through others, having them act as a director in your place, you would leave them personally liable themselves. You would also be in breach of a disqualification order that could in turn lead to imprisonment and fines.

The kinds of actions that can lead to disqualification include the following:

- *Trading while insolvent:* This occurs when your liabilities exceed your assets. At this point the shareholders' equity in the business has effectively ceased to exist and when shareholder equity is negative, directors are personally at risk and owe a duty of care to creditors – not shareholders. If you find yourself even approaching this area, you need the prompt advice of an insolvency practitioner. Directors who act properly will not be penalised and will live to fight another day. This was the situation in which the directors of many banks found themselves in the autumn of 2008.

- *Wrongful trading:* This can apply if, after a company goes into insolvent liquidation, the liquidator believes that the directors (or those acting as such) ought to have concluded earlier that the company had no realistic chance of survival. In these circumstances the courts can remove the shelter of limited liability and make directors personally liable for the company's debts.
- *Fraudulent trading:* This is rather more serious than wrongful trading. Here the proposition is that the director(s) were knowingly party to fraud on their creditors. The full shelter of limited liability can be removed in these circumstances.

A word of warning: despite the comforting sound of the prefix in the title, non-executive directors carry all the responsibilities of full-time directors even if they are not close enough to the business to know exactly what the true financial position is.

SHARING OUT THE SPOILS

When someone invests in a limited company or a public limited company (plc), they buy shares. These come in a number of different forms with differing rights and privileges. Both venture capitalists and business angels like to have a good leavening of preference shares for their investment. That ensures they can have their cake and eat it, often leaving only crumbs behind for other shareholders.

The types of shares are as follows:

- *Ordinary shares:* These form the bulk of the shares issued by most companies and carry the ordinary risks associated with being in business. All the profits of the business, including past retained profits, belong to the ordinary shareholders once any preference share dividends have been deducted. Ordinary shares have no fixed rate of dividend; indeed, over half the companies listed on US stock markets pay no or virtually no dividend. These include high-growth companies such as Google and Microsoft, which argue that by retaining and reinvesting all their profits they can create better value for shareholders than by distributing dividends. A company does not have to issue all its share capital at once. The total amount it is authorised to issue must be shown somewhere in the accounts, but only the issued share capital is counted in the balance sheet. Although shares can be partly paid, this is a rare occurrence.
- *Preference shares:* These get their name for two reasons. First, preference shareholders receive their fixed rate of dividend before ordinary shareholders. Second, in the event of a winding up of the company, any funds remaining go to repay preference share capital before any ordinary share capital. In a forced liquidation this may be of little comfort, as shareholders of any type come last in the queue after all other claims from creditors have been met.
- *Class A and class B:* These shares are issued where categories of shareholder are singled out for more or less favourable treatment in terms of control of the venture. Normally you might expect 51 per cent of the shares to outvote 49 per cent, but not always. For example, class A shares are often given up to five votes per share, while class B get one. In extreme cases class B shareholders can get no votes at all. Companies will often try to disguise the disadvantages associated with

owning shares with fewer voting rights by naming those shares. One of the most famous examples was their use by the Savoy Hotel Group to ward off an unwanted takeover by Trusthouse Forte. While Trusthouse was able to buy 70 percent of Savoy shares on the open market, it could only secure 42 per cent of the voting rights as it was only able to buy class B shares, the class A shares being in the hands of the Savoy family and its allies.

FINDING YOUR INVESTOR

There are two broad sources of equity: private equity, usually put in by individuals or small groups of individuals who for the prospects of greater returns will take on greater risks; or public capital through a share issue on a stock market. Only a very small handful of new or young ventures raise public money; more usually stock markets are where entrepreneurs and their backers realise their gains. Accordingly, we will be looking at this area in Chapter 14.

There are three main sources of private equity: business angels, venture capital firms and corporate venture funding. These all require that a company is formed to receive the invested funds, in return for which they will issue shares along the lines discussed earlier. They will also almost invariably insist on leveraging up their investment with a substantial pile of debt in various guises, but more on that in the next chapter.

Business Angels

One likely first source of equity or risk capital will be a private individual with his or her own funds, and perhaps some knowledge of your type of business. In return for a share in the business, such investors will put in money at their own risk. They have been christened 'business angels', a term first coined to describe private wealthy individuals who back a play on Broadway or in London's West End.

Most angels are determined on some involvement beyond merely signing a cheque and may hope to play a part in your business in some way. They are also hoping for big rewards. One angel who backed accounting software company Sage with £10,000 in its first round of £250,000 financing saw his stake rise to £40 million.

Business angels frequently operate through managed networks, usually on the Internet. In the UK and the US there are hundreds of networks, with tens of thousands of business angels prepared to put up several billion pounds each year into new or small businesses.

As they are investing their own money, business angels generally do less or even no due diligence; that is, checking up on you and the venture. They also can act very quickly, perhaps even writing an initial cheque on the day. To see business angels at work you need look no further than the BBC *Dragon's Den* series. The British Business Angels Association (www.bbaa.org.uk) has an online directory of UK business angels. The European Business Angels Network (www.eban.org) has directories of national business angel associations both inside and outside Europe, from which you can find individual business angels.

Venture Capital

Venture capitalists or VSs, sometimes unflatteringly referred to as vulture capitalists, are investing other people's money, often from pension funds. They have a different agenda from that of business angels and are more likely to be interested in investing more money for a larger stake. In general, VCs expect their investment to have paid off within seven years, but they are hardened realists. Two in every ten investments they make are total write-offs, and six perform averagely well at best. So, the one star in every ten has to cover a lot of duds. VCs have a target rate of return of 30 per cent plus to cover this poor hit rate.

Raising venture capital is not a cheap option and deals are not quick to arrange either. Six months is not unusual, and over a year has been known. Fees will run to hundreds of thousands of pounds, the sweetener being that these can be taken from the money raised.

You can find access to venture capital providers through the British Venture Capital Association (www.bvca.co.uk) and the European Venture Capital Association (www.evca.com). Both have online directories giving details of hundreds of venture capital providers. The Australian Government (www.austrade-ict.gov.au) has a global venture capital directory on its website and the National Venture Capital Association in the US (www.nvca.org) has directories of international venture capital associations both inside and outside the United States. You can see how those negotiating with or receiving venture capital rate the firm in question at The Funded (www.thefunded.com) in terms of the deal offered, the firm's apparent competence and how good it is at managing the relationship. There is also a link to the VC's website. The Funded has 2500 members.

Corporate Venturing

Mega corporations have an appetite for backing minnows. For instance, Sinclair Beecham and Julian Metcalfe, who started with a £17,000 loan and a name borrowed from a boarded-up shop when founding Pret A Manger, were not entrepreneurs content with doing their own thing. They had global ambitions and it was only by cutting in burger giant McDonald's that they could see any realistic way to dominate the world. In 2001 they sold a 33 per cent stake in their business for £25 million to McDonald's Ventures, a wholly owned subsidiary of McDonald's Corporation. They could also have considered Cisco, Apple Computers, IBM and Microsoft, which all have corporate venturing arms. Other corporate venturers include Deutsche Bank, which set up DB eVentures to get a window on the digital revolution; Reuters Greenhouse, which has stakes in 85 companies; even the late and unlamented Enron had venture investments (totalling $110 million). For an entrepreneur this approach can provide a 'friendly customer' and help open doors. For the 'parent' it provides a privileged ringside seat as a business grows and enables them to decide if the area is worth plunging into more deeply, or at the least provides valuable insights into new technologies or business processes.

Recent research into corporate venturing by Ashridge Management College (www.ashridge.org.uk) concluded that less than 5 per cent of corporate venturing units created new businesses that were taken up by the parent company. Moreover, many failed to make any positive contribution whatsoever. There are some success stories, however. In 2008 private equity firm Bridgepoint bought a majority stake in Pret A Manger, including McDonald's 33 per cent shareholding, for £345 million. That would suggest that McDonald's at least quadrupled the value of its initial stake. Nokia Venture Partners (NVP), which makes significant minority investments in start-ups in the wireless Internet space, had as its biggest success to date the Initial Public Offering of PayPal in 2002. At a conference in July 1999, NVP and Deutsche Bank used encryption technology owned by Paypal (then called Confinnity) to send founders Peter Thiel and Max Levchin $3 million in venture capital via a Palm Pilot as their initial stake.

Corporate venturing entrepreneurs think big and are happy to cut others with cash in on the deal, if it will help make them

Place du Caire
Deux 200 Sentier
Passage
Musée Cernavalet
Musée Baccarat

— Cristel

rich. Independence for independence's sake is not a high priority.

PRIVATE CAPITAL PRELIMINARIES

Two important stages will be gone through before a private investor will put cash into a business: the due diligence process, where an investor checks you and the business idea out to see if you are both as good as you claim; and the term sheet, where the split of ownership and the share categories and amounts are agreed. The emphasis put on these stages will vary according to the complexity of the deal, the amount of money involved and the legal ownership of the firms concerned. For example, a business angel investing on their own account can accept greater uncertainty on their own account than can a venture capital fund using a pension fund's money.

The Due Diligence Process

Usually, after a private equity firm signs a letter of intent to provide capital and you accept, it will conduct a due diligence investigation of both the management and the company. During this period the private equity firm will have access to all financial and other records, facilities, employees and so on to investigate before finalising the deal. The material to be examined will include copies of all leases, contracts and loan agreements in addition to copious financial records and statements. The investor will want to see any management reports, such as sales reports, inventory records, detailed lists of assets, facility maintenance records, aged receivables and payables reports, employee organisation charts, payroll and benefits records, customer records and marketing materials. It will want to know about any pending litigation, tax audits or insurance disputes. Depending on the nature of the business, it might also consider getting an environmental audit and an insurance check-up. The sting in the due diligence tail is that the current owners of the business will be required personally to warrant that everything they have said or revealed is both true and complete. In the event that proves not to be so, they will be personally liable to the extent of any loss incurred by those buying the shares.

The term sheet and what it means

A term sheet is a funding offer from a capital provider. It lays out the amount of an investment and the conditions under which the new investors expect the business owners to work using their money. The first page of the term sheet states the amount offered and the form of the funds (a bond – more about these in the next chapter – ordinary shares, preference shares or a combination of these). A price, either per £1000 unit of debt or per share of stock, is quoted to set the cost basis for investors getting in on your company. Later that starting price will be very important in deciding capital gains and any taxes due at acquisition, IPO (Initial Public Offering) or shares/units transferred.

Another key component of the term sheet is the 'post-closing capitalisation'. That is the proposed cash value of the venture on the day the terms are accepted. For example, investors may offer £500,000 in Series A preference shares at 50 pence per share (1 million shares) with a post-closing cap of £2 million. This translates into a 25 per cent ownership stake (£500,000 divided by £2 million).

The next section of the term sheet is typically a table that summarises the capital structure of your company. Investors generally start with preference shares in order to gain priority distribution should the enterprise fail and the liquidation of assets occur. The typical way to handle this is to have the preference shares convertible into ordinary shares on a 1:1 ratio at the investors' option, such that the preferred structure is essentially an ordinary share position, but with priority of repayment over the founders' own position.

Other terms included on the sheet could cover rents, equipment, levels of debt vs equity, minimum and maximum time periods associated with the transfer of shares, vesting in additional shares, option periods for making subsequent investments and having right of first refusal when other rounds of funding are sought in the future.

Hotmail – holding out for the best VC deal

In September 1988, Sabeer Bhatia arrived at Los Angeles International Airport. He had won a transfer scholarship to Cal Tech, scoring 62 out of 100 – the next highest score was 42. Sabeer intended to get his degrees and then to go home to work, probably as an engineer for a very large Indian company. He was following a modest path of life, like his parents. His mother was an accountant at the Central Bank of India for her entire career and his father spent 10 years as a captain in the Indian Army. But as a graduate student at Stanford, Sabeer was drawn to the basement of Terman auditorium. There, the speakers were entrepreneurs like Scott McNealy, Steve Wozniak and Marc Andreessen. Their fundamental message was always the same: 'You can do it too.'

When he graduated, Sabeer did not want to go home. So along with a fellow student, Jack Smith, he took a job at Apple Computer. Sabeer could have worked at Apple for 20 or 30 years, but he got swept up in the 1990s fever: you haven't lived until you've gone solo.

Sabeer met Farouk Arjani, a pioneer in the word-processing business in the 1970s and now a partner in Sequoia Ventures. The two hit it off and Arjani became Sabeer's mentor. In mid-1995, Sabeer began taking around a two-page executive summary business plan for a net-based personal database called JavaSoft. When Jack Smith, by now a partner in the venture – albeit a reluctant one – and Sabeer came up with the idea for Hotmail in December, JavaSoft effectively became the front for Hotmail.

Sabeer presented his business plan to Steve Jurvetson of Draper Fisher Jurvetson. Jurvetson remembers Sabeer's revenue estimates as showing that he was going to grow the company faster than any in history. After 20 outright rejections, Sabeer eventually got an offer from Draper Fisher Jurvetson of $300,000, with the venture capitalists retaining 30 per cent ownership, reasonable by industry standards. Sabeer held out for double that valuation, with the VCs' cut at 15 per cent. The negotiations got nowhere, so Sabeer shrugged, stood up and walked out of the door. His only other available option was a $100,000 'friends and family' round that had been arranged as back-up – not nearly enough money. If he had gone down that route, Hotmail wouldn't exist today. What actually happened was that Draper and Jurvetson relented; they called back the next day to accept 15 per cent.

On New Year's Eve just two years after writing the first draft of his business plan., Sabeer sold Hotmail to Microsoft in exchange for 2,769,148 of its shares. At that time those shares were worth $400 million. It was barely nine years since Sabeer had stepped off his flight from Bangalore, India with $250 in his pocket.

AFTER THE INVESTMENT, WHAT WILL YOUR BACKERS EXPECT?

Don't expect any investor to stay at home waiting for you to call them with an update on the progress of the business. They tend to be proactive and will almost certainly expect to put one, perhaps two directors onto your board. One will be the angel or a partner in the VC firm. They may also rope in a non-executive director from their pool of successful entrepreneurs or someone with special knowledge of relevance to your business or industry. These directors will expect to attend board meetings, usually once a month, and to be briefed beforehand. Monthly management accounts, forecasts, projections and updates on the business plan will all be essential.

As long as you are performing as per the plan, even if that plan means running up losses to the tune of several million pounds, all will be well. But once results stray far from the plan, and particularly if that looks like pushing the break-even date out significantly, expect the tempo to change. Your actions and plans will be probed, weekly and perhaps even daily. The investment funding will not all have been put up in one tranche, so the VC or angel will be able to exert powerful pressure. All along they will be trying hard to keep you believing that it's your business, but by now the reality will be sinking in. It will have become 'our' venture with you, in all probability, the junior partner, whatever it says on the share certificates, over the door or on the side of the vans.

That can be hard to take, but remember that professional investors bring not only money but also a huge amount of experience. You should therefore view their influence positively. They are there, after all, to help you achieve your goals for the business.

Chapter 7

Another day over and deeper in debt – leveraging the investment

Businesses have access to only two fundamentally different sorts of money: debt and equity. Super value ventures are plugged firmly into both, but it's important to understand the distinction between the two.

Equity, or owner's capital, including retained earnings, is money that is not a risk to the business. For instance, let's say that an angel invests £250,000 in your company in return for a 40 per cent equity stake. If the business is not doing well, there is no requirement to pay that investor anything. Put simply, if no profits are made, then the founder and other shareholders simply do not get dividends. The shareholders may not be pleased but they cannot usually sue, and even where they can sue the advisers who recommended the share purchase will be first in line.

Debt capital, on the other hand, is money borrowed by the business from outside sources; it puts the business at financial risk and is also risky for the lenders. In return for taking that risk they expect an interest payment every year, irrespective of the performance of the business.

However, what lenders do not usually expect is to share in the success of the venture. If you turn the £1 million borrowed from a bank into £10 million or £100 million (or more, as some of the entrepreneurs whose stories appear in this book have done), you still only have to repay that £1 million plus the agreed rate of interest. It's the ordinary shareholders who get to keep the lion's share of the booty.

Thus, lenders and investors have a different mindset. An angel or venture capitalist wants to take a share in a business that has the potential to grow, ultimately giving them a bigger return. Lenders, on the other hand, are primarily concerned with getting their money back.

Part of the assurance comes from knowing that the management is competent, but lenders will also cover their risks where they can by securing a charge against any assets the business or its managers may own. You can think of them as people who will help you turn a proportion of an illiquid asset such as equipment, property, stock-in-trade or customers who have not yet paid up, into a more liquid asset such as cash, but of course at some discount.

DEBT + EQUITY = GROWTH (POTENTIALLY)

It is common for growing companies to combine debt and equity funding and there are good reasons for doing so. However much money you and any partners or fellow investors are prepared to pump into your venture, it is unlikely to be sufficient backing for your business to realise its maximum value potential quickly or perhaps ever. But even though equity capital may be insufficient, without it any ability to raise large amounts of borrowed money is realistically zero.

Anyone considering a loan will want to see that you have enough faith in your proposition to back it with your own cash, however modest that may be. One rule applied here is 'the threshold of pain'. In other words, anyone putting money into your business wants to see that you will suffer too if it all goes wrong. So if you are worth a billion or two and you propose putting up a few tens of thousands yourself while inviting others to stump up millions, then expect short shrift.

The process of raising debt finance alongside equity is called leveraging and its role in raising investment and enhancing shareholder returns, while not exposing the business to undue risks, will be explained here. The debt-to-equity relationship is a movable feast. It varies with the type of organisation and the prevailing conditions in the money market. That ratio will be different for the same organisation at different times and when it is pursuing different strategies. Leveraging an inherently risky marketing strategy, say diversifying, with a risky financing strategy, using borrowed rather than shareholders' money, creates a potentially more risky situation than any one of those actions in isolation.

Leveraging the deal

First, let's get the jargon cleared up. In the US and almost any country outside the UK, leveraging is a term used to describe the relationship between the amount of debt capital in a business in proportion to that put in by shareholders. In the UK, gearing is more commonly used. The imagery that both terms seek to convey is that of a relatively small force being applied to greater effect. A large wheel cogged with a smaller one will make that wheel spin faster. Similarly, positioning a lever over a fulcrum so that more of it is on the side to which a force is being applied will make it possible to move a much heavier weight than otherwise.

Leveraging is a way to get more money into a venture than the shareholders are able or want to put up. In finance the term highly leveraged or highly geared describes the situation when a business has a high proportion of outside money to inside money. High leverage or gearing has considerable attractions to a business that wants to make high returns on shareholders' capital.

Bankers tend to favour a ratio of 1:1, that is equal amounts of debt and equity, as the maximum leverage for a business, although they have been known to go much higher. As well as looking at the gearing, lenders will study the business's capacity to pay interest. They do this by using another ratio called 'times interest earned'. This is calculated by dividing the operating profit by the loan interest. It shows how many times the loan interest is covered, and gives the lender some idea of the safety margin. The ratio for this example is given at the end of Table 7.1. Once again, rules are hard to make, but much less than three times interest earned is unlikely to give lenders confidence.

Miracle money

Table 7.1 shows an example of a business that is assumed to need £60,000 capital to generate £10,000 operating profits. Four different capital structures are considered. They range from all share capital (no leverage) at one end to nearly all loan capital at the other. The loan capital has to be 'serviced'; that is, interest of 12 per cent has to be paid. The loan itself can be relatively indefinite, simply being replaced by another one at market interest rates when the first loan expires.

Table 7.1 The effect of leverage on shareholders' returns

		No leverage N/A	Average leverage 1:1	High leverage 2:1	Very high leverage 3:1
Capital structure		£	£	£	£
Share capital		60,000	30,000	20,000	15,000
Loan capital (at 12%)		–	30,000	40,000	45,000
Total capital		60,000	60,000	60,000	60,000
Profits					
Operating profit		10,000	10,000	10,000	10,000
Less interest on loan		None	3,600	4,800	5,400
Net profit		10,000	6,400	5,200	4,600
Return on share capital	=	10,000	6,400	5,200	4,400
		60,000	30,000	20,000	15,000
	=	16.6%	21.3%	26%	30.7%
Times interest earned	=	N/A	10,000	10,000	10,000
			3,600	4,800	5,400
	=	N/A	2.8 times	2.1 times	1.8 times

Following the table through, you can see that return on the shareholders' money (arrived at by dividing the profit by the shareholders' investment and multiplying by 100 to get a percentage) grows from 16.6 to 30.7 per cent by virtue of the changed gearing. If the interest on the loan were lower, the ROSC, the term used to describe return on shareholders' capital, would be even more improved by high gearing; the higher the interest, the lower the relative improvement in ROSC. So in times of low interest rates, businesses tend to go for increased borrowings rather than raising more equity; that is, money from shareholders.

Are results from leveraging too good to be true?

At first sight this looks like a perpetual profit-growth machine. Naturally, shareholders, particularly venture capitalists and business angels as well as anyone else whose bonus depends on shareholders' returns, would rather have someone else 'lend' them the money for the business than ask shareholders for more money, especially if by doing so they increase the return on investment. The problem comes if the business does not produce £10,000 operating profits. Very often a drop in sales of 20 per cent means that profits are halved. If profits were halved in this example, the business could not meet the interest payments on its loan. That would make the business insolvent and so not in a 'sound financial position'; it would certainly be one that no one would want to lend money to. The next danger comes if the value of the equity against which the debt is being leveraged changes suddenly and substantially, for example if the value of a company's property assets or share price collapses. The lender will want to preserve the leverage ratio, say 1:1, but if the equity side drops the lender will want to claw back a similar proportion of the loan or ask for additional security.

THE UBIQUITOUS BANKS

Despite the seismic tremors that altered the banking world in 2008, banks are the principal source of money for all shapes and sizes of business. Firms around the world rely on banks for their funding in both the long and short term, for a number of important reasons. Despite the apparent speed with which large amounts of money can be deployed, for example when Lloyds Bank raised nearly $1 billion in a couple of days to help smooth the takeover of HBOS, that is very much the exception. Apart from business angels who are putting in their own cash, most sources of money except for the banks need weeks or months to agree finance.

The banks can generally move quickly for three reasons. First, they have been in the business a long time, far longer than any other source of funds, so their procedures are well established. Secondly, they have a strong retail presence, so they have in-depth knowledge of conditions on the ground for most types of industry. This gives them the confidence to make decisions and cuts out the research work that more distant financiers need to undertake. The final reason stems from that set out at the start of this chapter: banks look to secure their lending against business or personal assets, so in theory at least they are limiting their exposure to bad debts. In any event, a proportion of bad debts is written into their business model and charged out to all other borrowers. In the UK alone, banks provide around £65 billion to business customers, a good bit more than the £55 billion that firms have on deposit at any one time.

What are bank lenders looking for?

Bankers, and indeed any other sources of debt capital, are looking for asset security to back their loan and provide a near certainty of getting their money back. They will also charge an interest rate that reflects current market conditions and their view of the risk level of the proposal, usually anything from 0.25 per cent to upwards of 3 or 4 per cent for more risky or smaller firms.

Bankers like to speak of the 'five Cs' of credit analysis, the factors they look at when they evaluate a loan request. When applying to a bank for a loan, be prepared to address the following points:

• *Character:* Bankers lend money to borrowers who appear honest and who have a good credit history. Before you apply for a loan, it makes sense to obtain a copy of your credit report and clean up any problems.

- *Capacity:* This is a prediction of the borrower's ability to repay the loan. For a new business, bankers look at the business plan. For an existing business, bankers consider financial statements and industry trends.
- *Collateral:* Bankers generally want a borrower to pledge an asset that can be sold to pay off the loan if the borrower lacks funds.
- *Capital:* Bankers scrutinise a borrower's net worth, the amount by which assets exceed debts.
- *Conditions:* Whether bankers provide a loan can be influenced by the current economic climate as well as by the amount.

Types of bank funding

Although technically all the money that banks provide is in the form of loans, those loans come in a number of shapes and sizes. They all come with strings attached, other than the universal rule that they have at some point to be repaid, with interest. The rules, known in the trade as covenants, limit and define what you can do with the loan. For example, spending the loan on a new yacht rather than additional equipment or stock will go down very badly with your banker. If you do you will be deemed to be in breach of your covenants and so all bets will be off and the bank will be able to ask for its ten-year loan to be repaid immediately.

Overdrafts: The principal form of short-term bank funding is an overdraft, secured by a charge over the assets of the business. A little over a quarter of all bank finance for small firms is in the form of an overdraft. If you are starting out in a contract cleaning business, say, with a major contract, you need sufficient funds initially to buy the mop and bucket. Three months into the contract they will have been paid for, and so there is no point in getting a five-year bank loan to cover this, as within a year you will have cash in the bank and a loan with an early redemption penalty!

However, if your bank account does not get out of the red at any stage during the year, you will need to re-examine your financing. All too often companies utilise an overdraft to acquire long-term assets and that overdraft never seems to disappear, eventually constraining the business.

The attraction of overdrafts is that they are very easy to arrange and take little time to set up. That is also their inherent weakness. The key words in the arrangement document are 'repayable on demand', which leaves the bank free to make and change the rules as it sees fit. (This term is under continual review, and some banks may remove it from the arrangement.) With other forms of borrowing, as long as you stick to the terms and conditions, the loan is yours for the duration. It is not so with overdrafts.

Term loans: These are funds provided for a number of years. The interest can either be variable, changing with general interest rates, or fixed for a number of years ahead. The proportion of fixed-rate loans has increased from a third of all term loans to around one in two. In some cases it may be possible to move between having a fixed interest rate and a variable one at certain intervals. It may even be possible to have a moratorium on interest payments for a short period, to give the business some breathing space. Provided the conditions of the loan are met in such matters as repayment, interest and security cover, the money is available for the period of the loan. Unlike in the case of an overdraft, the bank cannot pull the rug from under you if circumstances (or the local manager) change. Just over a third of all term loans are for periods greater than ten years, and a quarter are for three years or less.

Government Small Firm Loan Guarantee Schemes: These are operated by banks at the instigation of governments in the UK, Australia, the US and elsewhere. These schemes guarantee loans from banks and other financial institutions for small businesses with viable business proposals that have tried and failed to obtain a conventional loan because of a lack of security. Loans are available for periods between two and ten years on sums from £5000 to £250,000.

The government guarantees 70–90 per cent of the loan. In return for the guarantee, the borrower pays a premium of 1–2 per cent a year on the outstanding amount of the loan. The commercial aspects of the loan are matters between the borrower and the lender.

Don't be too proud to grab a slice of government subsidised-cash. You will just be following in the footsteps of some great entrepreneurs. Tim Waterstone used the Small Firms Loan Scheme as part of his start-up funding, for example.

ASSET-BACKED FINANCE

Two other major sources of funds are less circumspect than banks when it comes to looking for security for money lent; indeed, their whole prospectus is predicated on a precise relationship between what a business has or will shortly have by way of assets, and what they are prepared to advance. Both groups play an important role in financing growing businesses.

Leasing

Physical assets such as cars, vans, computers, office equipment
and the like can usually be financed by leasing them, rather as
a house or flat may be rented. Alternatively, they can be bought
on hire purchase. This leaves other funds free to cover the less
tangible elements in your cash flow.

Leasing is a way of getting the use of vehicles, plant and
equipment without paying the full cost all at once. Operating
leases are taken out where you will use the equipment (for
example a car, photocopier, vending machine or kitchen equipment) for less than its full economic life. The lessor takes the
risk of the equipment becoming obsolete, and assumes responsibility for repairs, maintenance and insurance. As you, the
lessee, are paying for this service, it is more expensive than a
finance lease, where you lease the equipment for most of its
economic life and maintain and insure it yourself. Leases can
normally be extended, often for fairly nominal sums, in the
latter years.

Hire purchase differs from leasing in that you have the option
eventually to become the owner of the asset, after a series of
payments.

You can find a leasing company via the Finance and Leasing
Association's Business Finance Directory (www.fla.org), which
gives details of all UK-based businesses offering this type of
finance. The website also has general information on terms of
trade and code of conduct.

Discounting and Factoring

Customers often take time to pay up. In the meantime you have
to pay those who work for you and your less patient suppliers.
So the more you grow, the more funds you need. However, it
is often possible to 'factor' your creditworthy customers' bills to

a financial institution, receiving some of the funds as your goods leave the door, hence speeding up cash flow.

Factoring is generally only available to a business that invoices other business customers, either in its home market or internationally, for its services. Factoring can be made available to new businesses, although its services are usually of most value during the early stages of growth. It is an arrangement that allows you to receive up to 80 per cent of the cash due from your customers more quickly than they would normally pay. The factoring company in effect buys your trade debts, and can also provide a debtor accounting and administration service. You will, of course, have to pay for factoring services. If you have more good customers than you can afford to sell to, then factoring could be a useful tool.

Having the cash before your customers pay will cost you a little more than normal overdraft rates. The factoring service will cost between 0.5 and 3.5 per cent of the turnover, depending on the volume of work, the number of debtors, the average invoice amount and other related factors. You can get up to 80 per cent of the value of your invoice in advance, with the remainder paid when your customer settles up, less the various charges just mentioned.

However, if you sell direct to the public, sell complex and expensive capital equipment or expect progress payments on long-term projects, factoring is not for you. Nevertheless, if you are expanding more rapidly than other sources of finance will allow, this may be a useful service that is worth exploring.

Invoice discounting is a variation on the same theme where you are responsible for collecting the money from debtors; this is not a service available to new or very small businesses. You can find an invoice discounter or factor through the Asset Based Finance Association (www.thefda.org.uk), representing the UK's 41 factoring and invoice discounting businesses.

BONDS, DEBENTURES AND MORTGAGES

Bonds, debentures and mortgages are all kinds of borrowing with different rights and obligations for the parties concerned. For a business, a mortgage is much the same as for an individual. The loan is for a specific event, buying a particular property asset such as a factory, office or warehouse. Interest is payable and the loan itself is secured against the property, so should the business fail the mortgage can substantially be redeemed.

Companies wanting to raise funds for general business purposes other than property issue debentures or bonds. These run for a number of years, typically three years and upwards, with the bond or debenture holder receiving interest over the life of the loan, with the capital returned at the end of the period.

The key difference between debentures and bonds lies in their security and ranking. Debentures are unsecured and so in the event of the company being unable to pay interest or repay loans, the lender may well get little or nothing back. Bonds are secured against specific assets and so rank ahead of debentures for any pay-out. Unlike bank loans that are usually held by the issuing bank (although even that assumption is being challenged by an escalation in the securitisation of debt being packaged up and sold on), bonds and debentures are sold to the public in much the same way as shares. The interest demanded will be a factor of the prevailing market conditions and the financial strength of the borrower.

Saga – a roller-coaster of finance deals

The name that is synonymous with providing holidays exclusively for the over-50s is undoubtedly Saga. The business started out in 1951 with the daunting name of Old People's Travel Bureau as an experiment by Folkestone hotelier Sidney De Haan. He believed that older holidaymakers would appreciate a quieter off-season break by the sea. Initially charging just £6.10s, including travel, full board and three excursions, over the next decade the company grew rapidly into chartering trains, planes and finally buying its own boat, the *Saga Rose*. Along the way it launched a magazine, an insurance business and a clutch of FM radio stations. Over a third of the UK's over-50s are on Saga's database, which holds 7 million individuals of whom over 2 million actively buy from Saga each year. By 2007 the company was making £158.2 million in profits and employing 3800 people worldwide.

The company's financing history has been something of a roller-coaster. Initially it was financed using family money and bank debt. The firm was floated on the stock market in 1978 but was not a hit with investors, partly because of a weakening UK holiday market. The De Haan family took the group private in 1990, buying out all the other investors. By 2004 the company was preparing to go back onto the stock market when the private equity firm, Charterhouse Capital Partners, paid £1.35 billion to take control of the group. The acquisition was by way of a buy-out, with Charterhouse taking an 80 per cent stake and Saga's management the remainder. Charterhouse funded the acquisition with £500 million of equity. The remainder was funded with debt, which it has since refinanced.

119

In 2007, just three years later, the company, then thought to be worth between £2.5 billion and £3 billion, was again exploring its financing strategy. A sale or flotation could value the 20 per cent stake held by staff and senior management at £500 million, with the 8 per cent stake of Andrew Goodsell, Saga's chief executive, worth about £200 million. Mr Goodsell stated, 'We've smashed through all of our plans, repaid large amounts of debt and [Charterhouse] has achieved what it wanted to achieve.' Once again stock-market flotation was on the cards, but a very different opportunity emerged. In June 2007 Permira and CVC, the two private equity firms that owned the bulk of the AA, approached Saga's majority owner Charterhouse to ask it to consider a merger. The result was a £6.15 billion surprise move that created one of the country's largest private equity-backed companies.

Ultimately, debt and private equity finance is a means to an end. Or to put it another way, it is the necessary lubricant that will provide your business with the support it needs to deliver on its business plan and take advantage of the growth opportunities in the market.

So with the finance in place, it's time to look at the strategies that will enable you grow your business. In the next part of the book, we look at how you get big.

GET BIG

Chapter 8

You must be this high to go on the ride – why babies can't swim

If you want to get seriously rich rather than simply run a lifestyle business that delivers an income, then you need to think in terms of getting big – and that means growing your market share.

It's a simple enough equation. When the time comes to sell your business, the amount you can expect to get will be to a greater or lesser extent based on a multiple of profits. And the truth is that profitability tends to be linked very closely with size in the market.

The facts are there to support this claim. In 1960, the vice president of marketing services at technology and services giant GE initiated a large-scale project to examine the profit impact of marketing strategies. Decades of computer number crunching produced a model that identified the major factors responsible for a great deal of the variation in a business's ROI (return on investment). Later the project, now known as PIMS (Profit

Impact of Marketing Strategies), moved to a non-profit organisation associated with the Harvard Business School and is now based at the Strategic Planning Institute (www.pimsonline.com). Information has been gathered from over 3000 participating businesses in the form of about 200 pieces of data on each business. The PIMS database covers businesses of every shape, size and business sector around the globe.

The research has produced two compelling facts. First, most of the strategic factors that boost ROI also contribute to the long-term value of a business. Secondly, market share and profitability are strongly related. Businesses with very large market shares, over 50 per cent, have rates of return more than three times greater than those with under 10 per cent of their markets. The primary reason for the market share–profitability link, apart from the connection with relative quality, is that businesses that are big relative to their competitors benefit from economies of scale and so have lower unit costs than their smaller competitors.

VALUE ON EXIT

That brings us back to value. Small businesses are worth disproportionately less than bigger ones when sold. Table 8.1 shows the multiples achieved on average by small private companies when sold, compared with businesses in a similar sector listed on the AIM (Alternative Investment Market) and the LSE (London Stock Exchange). In effect, each £1 million of profit generated by a small firm would be valued at £4 million on exit and at £12 million were the company large, with sales in excess of £100 million per annum. (We will look at these terms in Chapter 14.)

Table 8.1 Multiples on sale

Company Average	P/E
Private with turnover up to £10 million	4
AIM listed with turnover up to £50 million	6.5
Full market listed company with turnover in excess of £100 million	12

WHY SIZE MEANS SAFETY

There are other reasons to get big – not least safety. In recent years we have all seen that some businesses are considered too big to be allowed to fail. Aside from Lehman Brothers, at the time of writing no major western bank had gone bust during the biggest credit crunch since the 1929 depression, though arguably all bar a handful deserved to. The big US and European motor manufacturers were rescued when sales plunged by nearly a third in the last quarter of 2008. But even businesses not quite in the super league have a measure of protection by virtue of their size.

Let's suppose that a business in its first year's trading wins ten customers, generating sales of £1 million. To keep things simple, we will assume that they all buy the same amount. If any one customer goes bust or defaults on paying, the firm stands to lose £100,000. In a bad year that could well happen and if it did there would be a hole in the firm's finances equivalent to a whole year's profits, as businesses this size typically make 10 per cent profit on sales. Roll forward a year or so and the same business has a turnover of £10 million from 100 customers making £1 million annual profits. Losing a customer to the competition, or worse still having one go bust owing you money, would be unpleasant. You would be £100,000 (10 per cent of profits) down, a survivable position. You would have to lose ten customers, an extremely unlikely event if your credit controller and sales manager are on the ball, before you were wiped out. So the more customers you have, the less important – and dangerous – losing one or two will be.

BUILDING A TEAM AS THE BUSINESS GROWS

Larger businesses also tend to have not only bigger management teams, but also management structures that allow the entity to continue to function successfully long after the founder has gone. Investors like this and the reason is simple. They know that no super entrepreneur wants to stay on too long after their business has been sold, so the key to releasing value lies in having a management team to remain and run the business. However, to be effective and realise its full potential the business needs management in depth. That gives a business several major benefits in the quest for value:

- There is cover in the event of illness, or worse. A business with just the founder and a couple of managers could be knocked back years if one person is unavailable for whatever reason for any more than a week or two.
- There is a cadre of people to promote from as the business grows. Growing your own management is one of the surest ways to get people who fit the culture and ethos.
- There are enough people to generate a meaningful debate about strategy and tactics. Small groups rapidly become incestuous and stale. Having a wide pool of talent to draw on for ideas, inspiration and knowledge is a common ingredient of high-flying businesses.

But if size is a good thing, how do you go about scaling up?

How Flowcrete built a team

Dawn Gibbons, co-founder of Flowcrete (www.flow-crete.com), has taken her company from a 400 sq ft unit (the size of a double garage) with £2000 capital to a plc with a turnover of €52 million in the field of floor-screeding technology and clients including household names such as Cadbury, Sainsbury's, Unilever, Marks & Spencer, Barclays and Ford. Flowcrete's initial success was down to a continuing focus on technical superiority. This attribute was engendered by Dawn's father, a well-respected industrial chemist with an interest in resin technology.

But arguably, Dawn's skills contributed as much if not more to the firm's success. 'We want to be champions of change,' Gibbons claims. She has built up a strong management team that has made it possible for her company to adapt rapidly to the fast-changing business environment she faces.

The firm has restructured a dozen times, focusing on new trends brought about by its customers' changing needs. The first reappraisal came after seven years in business, when Flowcrete realised that its market was no longer firms that laid floors; it now had to become an installer itself. Changes in the market meant that to maintain growth Flowcrete had to appoint proven specialist contractors, train its staff, write specifications and carry out audits to ensure quality.

Chapter 9

The path to growth – and riches too

On the face of it, the path to growth and a bright future for your company is a simple one. You sell more products, increase market share and in doing so create a more profitable and valuable company. However, once we begin to look more closely at the concept of 'market share', it quickly becomes apparent that you shouldn't necessarily be thinking in terms of a single or supposedly homogeneous customer base. Indeed, to fulfil your company's growth potential, you should be looking closely at how your customer base breaks down, why sub-groups within that target audience are buying your products, and how best you can deliver products or services that meet the requirements of those segments.

SEGMENTING YOUR MARKET

Think of it this way. At a corporate level General Motors and Ford are vehicle manufacturers, but that actually doesn't tell you much about the companies themselves or their customers. The reality is that both groups make everything from heavy-duty commercial vehicles, through luxury SUVs to very small or ecologically sound vehicles such as hybrids or electric cars, and they sell these to different customers with different requirements.

A company doesn't have to be big or global to be operating in very different business sectors. For example, a small carpet and upholstery cleaning business could have private individuals who need their homes spring cleaned and business clients running restaurants and guesthouses. These two segments are fundamentally different, one more focused on cost and the other more concerned that the work is carried out with the least disruption to their business. Also, each of these customer groups is motivated to buy for different reasons and the service, price and selling message will in all probability need to be modified to strike a chord with each.

Having customers with different needs means that we need to organise our marketing effort to address each kind of customer individually. Trying to satisfy everyone may mean that we end up satisfying no one fully. The marketing process that helps us deal with this seemingly impossible task is market segmentation. This is the name given to the process of organising customers and potential customers into clusters or groups of similar types.

Segmenting your market ensures that you have a better chance of delighting customers, as your offers appear more tailored than they might otherwise be. It also allows you to focus on capturing high market share in several smaller market segments where you are less likely to have to compete head on with big, established competitors. Upsetting the big boys can be a painful experience.

Types of market segments

These are some of the most popular ways to divide up markets:

- *Geographic segmentation:* This is when companies present their products and services differently in different countries or regions. At its simplest this could involve translating literature or pricing similar products differently. A recent example is Google's G1 mobile phone, launched in 2008 and priced higher in Europe than in the US, reflecting the difference in both cost structures and competitive environment.

- *Benefit segmentation:* This approach recognises that different people can get different satisfaction from the same product or service. Lastminute.com claims two quite distinctive benefits for its users. First, it aims to offer people bargains that appeal because of price and value. Secondly, the company has recently been laying more emphasis on the benefit of immediacy. This idea is rather akin to the impulse-buy products placed at checkout tills, which you never thought of buying until you bumped into them on your way out.

- *Psychographic segmentation:* Here individual consumers are divided into social groups such as 'Yuppies' (young, upwardly mobile professionals), 'Bumps' (borrowed-to-the-hilt, upwardly mobile, professional show-offs) and 'Jollies' (jet-setting oldies with lots of loot). These categories try to show how social behaviour influences buyer behaviour. The most infamous of these categories is 'ninja' borrowers – no income, no job, no assets – who were tempted into home ownership, particularly in the US, with interest rates of 1 per cent, but which they had no serious hope of paying when rates later peaked at 5.25 per cent.

- *Industrial segmentation:* Here commercial customers are grouped together according to a combination of their geographic location, principal business activity, relative size, frequency of product use, buying policies and a range of other factors.

- *Multivariant segmentation:* This occurs where several variables are used to give a more precise picture of a market than using just one factor alone.

Deciding how to segment your market

These are four useful rules to help decide if a market segment is worth trying to sell into:

- *Measurability:* Can you estimate how many customers are in the segment? Are there enough to make it worth offering them something different?
- *Accessibility:* Can you communicate with these customers, preferably in a way that reaches them on an individual basis? For example, you could reach the over-50s by advertising in a specialist 'older people's' magazine with reasonable confidence that younger people will not read it. So if you were trying to promote Scrabble with tiles 50 per cent larger, you might prefer that young people did not hear about it. If they did, it might give the product an old-fashioned image.
- *Open to profitable development:* The customers must have money to spend on the benefits that you propose to offer. A good example here is the emergence of the halal food market segment. It is only in the last few years that major companies have seen this as profitable. By 2008 Nestlé had gone halal in 75 of its 480 plants worldwide to meet the surge in demand for food and products acceptable to devout Muslims. With McDonald's, Tesco and Sainsbury all entering the halal sector too, what had been a nice little earner for the locals looks set to change hands.
- *Size:* A segment has to be large enough to be worth your exploiting it, but perhaps not so large as to attract larger competitors.

MASTERING THE MATRIX

Segmenting markets is a great starting point in your quest for growth, but it will in all probability leave you with more questions than answers. There are thousands of potential options, but which should you choose and why? Are some strategies more likely to succeed than others?

Igor Ansoff, while professor of Industrial Administration at the Graduate School at Carnegie Mellon University, developed a way of categorising strategies as an aid to understanding the nature of the risks involved. He invited his students to consider growth options as a square matrix divided into four segments. The axis are labelled with products and services running along the 'x' axis, starting with 'present' and 'new'; and markets up the 'y' axis, similarly labelled. Ansoff went on to assign titles to each type of strategy, in an ascending scale of risk:

- *Market penetration:* Selling more of your existing products and services to existing customers – the lowest-risk strategy.
- *Product/service development:* Creating extensions to your existing products or new products to sell to your existing customer base. This is more risky than market penetration, but less risky than entering a new market where you will face new competitors and may not understand the customers as well as you do your current ones.
- *Market development:* Entering new market segments or completely new markets, either in your home country or abroad.
- *Diversification:* Selling new products into new markets; the most risky strategy as both are relative unknowns. To be avoided unless all other strategies have been exhausted. Diversification can be further subdivided into four

categories of increasing risk profile: horizontal diversification (entirely new product into current market); vertical diversification (move backwards into firm's supplier or forward into customer's business); concentric diversification (new product closely related to current products either in terms of technology or marketing presence but into a new market); conglomerate diversification (completely new product into a new market).

You can find out more about the Ansoff matrix at www.strategyvectormodel.com.

How to milk your customer base

Let's take a closer look at the options presented to you by the matrix. The greatest opportunities for rapid, profitable and low-cost growth lie in extending and developing your relationship with your existing customers. These are some of the areas to explore that won't break the bank.

Generate referrals

The chances are that your existing customers know others like themselves, who in turn know yet more potential customers. You will know from your own experience that if anyone talks in glowing terms about a restaurant, cleaner, babysitter or website designer they have recently used, a long queue will form to get their contact details. The maths here are impressive. Delighted customers tell up to ten others, so once the ball is rolling it can quickly gather momentum. The American Customer Satisfaction Index (www.acsi.org) measures satisfaction in 43 industries. Checking the score for your industry will give you a benchmark to aim for in order to increase your chance of improving the number of referrals you can secure.

Review lost orders

There will be plenty of occasions when you don't get an order, but that needn't be a dead loss. There is valuable information that can be gleaned from the experience if you take the time to find out why the order was lost. One company, a secondhand Internet bookseller, discovered that the cost of shipping the product was the single most important reason for an enquiry not being converted into an order. Its costs were out of line with others in the market because it had adopted a single price strategy that lumped heavy big books and small light ones together into a single price band; this was administratively easy but a marketing disaster, as a book costing less than £1 ended up costing five times that figure when delivery was taken into account. Once the firm knew why it was losing business, it changed its strategy and started winning more business. The maths here are also an eye opener. Dissatisfied customers tell 19 others of their bad experience and, worse still, 96 per cent of complaints don't get reported, the customer just walks!

Retain more customers

Acquiring customers is an expensive process: they have to be found, wooed and won. Once you have them onside they cost less to keep, spend more money with you and are less price sensitive than new customers. Retaining customers will do more than almost any other marketing strategy to grow your profit margin. According to customer loyalty research carried out by Bain (www.bain.com), a 5 per cent increase in customer retention can improve profitability by 75 per cent.

Beat competitors

Having gone to all the trouble of winning and retaining a customer, it makes good sense to get that customer to buy more. Usually this brings you, the supplier, economies in administration costs and delivery charges; also as a known entity, existing customers can usually be relied on to pay up. But before you can get them to buy more, you need to know how much they do or could buy and who else, if anyone, they buy from; in other words, who you are in competition with. This is back to having good intelligence on your customers. You can find out who else supplies them and what their annual purchase quantities will be by including a question on competitors in your next satisfaction questionnaire. As for how much they buy, usually you can rely on market averages.

Next, you need to devise a strategy to win that extra business from your customers. Offering a three-for-two discount, free delivery if they order three or some such strategy would mean giving up some part of your additional profit, but still ending up with more profit than if you had settled for just a one-pack order.

Convert non-users

There are inevitably many non-users of whatever you and your competitors sell. For example, while over 60% per cent of UK households are online, that means 40 per cent are not. AOL's strategy here is encapsulated in its 'Do a friend a favour' campaigns. Sending disks to existing customers with the message 'Get your friend on line with AOL and once both you and your friend have been on line for 60 days or more you will receive £30 FREE', AOL hoped that a proportion would remain as customers.

Create new products and services for your present customers

Most new product launches by big businesses don't succeed and in the grocery business the failure rate is over 75 per cent. While that figure may sound alarming, you have to offset against that the cost of development, which if low may not be a problem, and the rewards of success. Google's two dozen new product launches in the four years to 2006, including Google Talk, Google Finance and Gmail, have yet to become serious players, ranking around 40th in their respective markets with no more than 2 per cent market shares. Google's strategy of launching early and often means that glitches are accepted, but its aim is to encourage its geeks to take risks and stay creative, knowing that the pay-off when they get a winner will be colossal.

By far the easiest strategy here is to ask your customers what they want. Samantha Buriton, founder of SoOrganic (www.soorganic.com), did lots of research on her customers in launching the 1200 products the company now sells online. Her website has an e-mail address and phone number for customers to contact the business with ideas or suggestions for products to be included in the range. Her product promise is that she will only list products she would be happy to recommend to her friends. (Buriton's use of public relations also makes for interesting reading – hit the 'IN THE PRESS' tab at the top of the page.)

LIVING WITH LIFE CYCLES

Ansoff's Matrix may help with weighing up the risks of a particular growth strategy, but it doesn't tell us much about what might happen once it is implemented. If you think that all products and services have their moment in the sun and then fade into near oblivion like a shooting star, there is a strong body of business theory to support you. The idea that business products and services have a life cycle much like any being was first

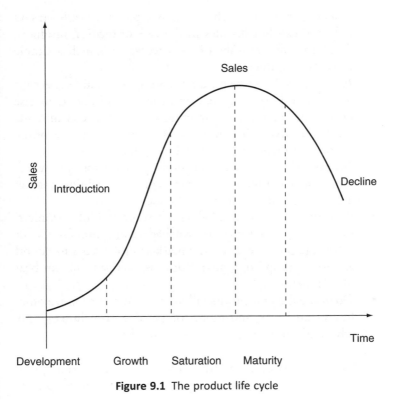

Figure 9.1 The product life cycle

137

seen in management literature as far back as 1922, when researchers looking back at the growth of the US automobile industry observed a bell-shaped pattern in sales of individual cars. Over the following four decades various practitioners and researchers adding, substituting and renaming the stages in the life cycle arrived at the five steps in Figure 9.1. The length of a product's lifetime can be weeks or months in the case of a fad such as the mass of ineffective and often dangerous exercise machines that are rushed out in response to any medical claim, for example on the value of reducing core fat.

- *Product development:* This stage is typified by cash outlays only and can last decades in the case of medical products, down to a few months or even weeks to launch a simple consumer product.
- *Introduction:* Here the product is brought to market, perhaps just to one initial segment and the activity may comprise little more than a test marketing activity. Once again costs are high; advertising and selling costs have to be borne upfront and sales revenues will be minimal.
- *Growth:* This stage sees the product sold across the whole range of a company's market segments, gaining market acceptance and becoming profitable.
- *Maturity and saturation:* Sales peak as the limit of customers' capacity to consume is reached and competitors or substitute products enter the market. Profit starts to tail off as prices drop and advertising is stepped up to beat off competitors.
- *Decline:* Sales and profits fall away as competition becomes heavy and better and more competitive or technologically advanced products come into the market.

The usefulness of the product life cycle as a marketing tool is as an aid to deciding on the appropriate strategy to adopt. For example, at the introduction stage the goal for advertising and promotion may be to inform and educate; during the growth stage differences need to be stressed to keep competitors at bay; during maturity customers need to be reminded that you are still around and it's time to buy again. During decline, it is probable that advertising budgets could be cut and prices lowered. As all major costs associated with the product will have been covered at this stage, it should still be profitable.

These of course are only examples of possible strategies rather than rules to be followed. For example, many products are successfully relaunched during the decline stage by changing an element of the marketing mix or being repositioned into a different marketplace. Cigarette manufacturers are responding to declining markets in developed economies by targeting markets such as Africa and China, even setting up production there and buying up local brands to extend their range of products.

UNDERSTANDING ADOPTERS – WHO BUYS YOUR PRODUCTS AND WHEN

Whichever growth strategy you end up pursuing, you can be pretty certain that sales will not take off like wildfire. So what can you read into the apparent indifference of customers to your wonderful new product or your arrival in their market? The basic rule here is 'don't panic'. Word spreads slowly as the message is diffused throughout the various customer groups. Even then it is noticeable that generally it is the more adventurous types who buy first from a new business. Only after these people have given their seal of approval do the 'followers' come along. Research shows that this adoption process, as it is known, moves through five distinct customer characteristics, from innovators to laggards, with the overall population being different for each group (see Table 9.1 below).

Table 9.1 The product/service adoption cycle

Innovators	2.5% of the overall market
Early adopters	13.5% of the overall market
Early majority	34.0% of the overall market
Late majority	34.0% of the overall market
Laggards	16.0% of the overall market
Total market	100%

Let's suppose you have identified a new market for your product aimed at affluent professionals. It only makes economic sense to service these customers within a ten-mile radius of your base. So if market research shows that there are 100,000 people that meet the profile of your ideal customer, the market open for exploitation at the outset may be as low as 2500 people, which is the 2.5 per cent of innovators. And you may only get a few hundred of them in the early weeks and months. So though your market appears relatively big, only a small fraction of that is likely to think about buying quickly.

This adoption process, from the 2.5 per cent of innovators who make up a new business's first customers through to the laggards who won't buy from anyone until it has been in business for 20 years, is most noticeable with truly innovative and relatively costly goods and services, but the general trend is true for all businesses. Until you have sold to the innovators, significant sales cannot be achieved. So an important first task is to identify these customers. The moral is: the more you know about your potential customers at the outset, the better your chances of success.

One further issue to keep in mind when shaping your marketing strategy is that innovators, early adopters and all the other sub-segments don't necessarily use the same media, websites, magazines and newspapers or respond to the same images and messages. So they need to be marketed to in very different ways.

MIXING WITH THE MARKET – WHAT DOES YOUR COMPANY BRING TO THE PARTY?

A cook can take the same or similar ingredients in different proportions and produce very different dishes. In much the same way, a change in business ingredients can produce an offering tailored to meet the needs of a specific market segment. The ingredients with which marketing strategy can be developed and implemented are price, product (and/or service), promotion and place. A fifth 'P', people, is often added. The term 'marketing mix' has a pedigree going back to the late 1940s when marketing managers first referred to mixing ingredients to create strategies. E. Jerome McCarthy, a marketing professor at Michigan State University in 1960, initially formalised the concept.

Product/service

When the term marketing mix was first coined, the bulk of valuable trade was concerned with physical goods. Certainly services existed, but these were mostly supplied by professions such as law, accountancy, insurance and finance, where the concept of marketing was in any event taboo. Today a product is generally accepted as the whole bundle of 'satisfactions', either tangible such as a physical product, or intangible such as warranties, guarantees or customer support, which support that product. The bundle that makes up a successful product or service includes:

- Design
- Specification and functionality

- Brand name/image
- Performance and reliability
- Quality
- Safety
- Packaging
- Presentation and appearance
- After-sales service
- Availability
- Delivery
- Colour/flavour/odour/touch
- Payment terms

Price

Seemingly the simplest of the marketing choices, price is often the most agonising decision you will be faced with. The subject transcends almost every area of a business. The economists get the ball rolling with ideas around the elasticity of demand. Set too high a price and no one comes to the dance; too low and your budget for bouncers will go off the Richter scale. However profitable a certain price may be for the business, it may just be so low that it devalues other products in your range.

High price may also be used as a strategy. Apple, for example, has a position fairly and squarely at the innovator end of the product adoption cycle. Its customers expect to pay high prices for the privilege of being the first users of a new product. The iPod was positioned above the Walkman in price terms, though as the market for pocket sound devices was already mature there was scope to come into the market lower down the price spectrum.

Promotion and advertising

The answers to the following five questions underpin all advertising and promotional strategies:

1. *What do you want to happen?* This needs to be a specific outcome, such as getting prospective customers to visit your website; phone, write or e-mail you; return a card, or send an order in the post.
2. *If that happens how much is it worth?* Once you know what you want a particular promotional activity to achieve, it becomes a little easier to estimate its cost. Suppose a £1000 advertisement is expected to generate 100 enquiries for your product. If experience tells you that on average 10 per cent of enquiries result in orders, and your profit margin is £200 per product, then you can expect an extra £2000 profit. That 'benefit' is much greater than the £1000 cost of the advertisement, so it seems a worthwhile investment.
3. *What message will make it happen?* This should be built around facts about the company and about the product. It is worth remembering that your customers are only interested in the facts that influence their buying decisions; in other words, what's in it for them and how your business and its products stand out from the competition.
4. *What media will work best?* Research (see Chapter 4) should produce a clear understanding of who constitutes your potential customer group and so provide pointers for how to reach them. But even when you know those facts, it is not always plain sailing. Advertising in the *Fishing Times*, for example, will be effective at reaching fishermen but less so at reaching their partners, who might be persuaded to buy them fishing tackle for Christmas or birthdays. Also the *Fishing Times* will be jam packed with competitors' adverts. It might just be worth considering a Web ad on a page giving Tide Tables to avoid going head to head with competitors or getting into a gift catalogue to grab that market's attention.
5. *How will you measure the effectiveness of your effort and expense?* If you have done your work in assessing what it is worth to

you to advertise (see point 2 above), you have the answer to this question.

Place

This aspect of marketing strategy is about how products and services actually get into the customer's hands. If you are a retailer, restaurant or hotel chain, for example, then your customers will come to you. Here your physical location will most probably be the key to success. For businesses in the manufacturing field, it is more likely that you will go out to find customers. In this case it will be your channels of distribution that are the vital link.

GOING GLOBAL

Extending into global markets is one of the most successful growth strategies that until the advert of the Internet was the prerogative of big, established businesses. However, many small and new businesses have now found that you can leverage small market segments around the world and combine them into a very substantial market for relatively esoteric offers such as hotel toiletries for five-star hotels. There are only a few score such hotels in Pacific's home market, but around the world there are thousands, and more still if the concept is stretched to anywhere else luxurious where you may spend the night – aircraft and cruise liners, for example.

Pacific Direct – Building a global market

Pacific Direct, which we met in Chapter 5, did not exactly represent an obvious candidate for globalisation. The niche founder Lara Morgan spotted was in providing hotel toiletries, an industry in its infancy when she started out. Soon she realised that to be competitive she would have to find low-cost manufacturing facilities. She identified China as the best place to get miniature plastic containers, disposable slippers, dressing gowns and other related products that go into a complete hotel bathroom package. As the contents of the toiletries bottles were supplied from the UK, France and the US, it made no economic sense to ship those out to China, so the bottles were brought back to the UK for filling. Soon Lara found a better solution using a supplier in the Czech Republic which pitched a competitive price.

On the back of a low-cost structure, Lara rapidly identified five-star hotels as the area to focus on. They were not too price sensitive and the opportunity to get good profit margins was significantly better than in the more cost-conscious lower-grade hotels. Starting with the Dorchester Hotel in Park Lane, London, Lara built up sales with international five-star hotels, cruise ships, airlines and resorts around the world. Once she had penetrated her five-star niche market she was able to extend her product range and build up a unique offer.

Both the Chinese and Czech businesses needed money to expand so that they could keep up with Lara's rapid growth, so she took majority stakes in both, offering credit to help them stay in the game. As well as running a business with a multimillion-pound turnover, Lara has ensured that Pacific Direct puts something back to the societies where she operates. The company works with local Bedford hospices and the Morning Star Orphanage in Nepal, and does not test products on animals.

Choosing your overseas markets

Finding the optimal country to locate a new venture in or to find suppliers and business partners in involves researching the political and economic environment of the country concerned and its attitude to enterprise. You will also need to take stock of your own appetite for risk. For example, although buying into a factory in China and employing 400 staff sounds an adventurous, even dangerous strategy for someone living in Bedford, as Lara speaks fluent Mandarin and spent her childhood in Hong Kong it was not as risky as it seemed.

Some regions and countries are probably just too risky for any but the desperate to try, although at the time of writing one enterprising Brit is setting up a property business in Kabul (Afghanistan). Apparently on the back of meteoric growth fuelled by the influx of aid workers and consultants, houses in desirable areas of town go for $500,000.

Using the following sources you can keep track of the countries where you can have a reasonable chance of both being welcome and prospering. They will help you to get a quick appreciation of your prospects in overseas markets around the world:

Doing Business (www.doingbusiness.org): This is a World Bank Group website that assesses and measures business regulations and their enforcement across 175 countries. Its indicators identify specific regulations that enhance or constrain business investment, productivity and growth and provide yardsticks to gauge how welcoming a country is towards entrepreneurs. The topics include starting a business; closing a business; paying taxes; dealing with licences; employing workers; registering property; getting credit; protecting investors; trading across borders and enforcing contracts.

Central Intelligence Agency (CIA) World Factbook (www.cia.gov): This has a wealth of information, sufficient to form a view

THE PATH TO GROWTH – AND RICHES TOO

on the economic health, or otherwise, of a particular country. The CIA keeps the Factbook up to date on a regular basis throughout the year, providing the most current information to hand. Once in the Factbook you are offered a pull-down bar in the top left of the screen, which allows you to select any of the 233 countries or regions afforded separate status for analytical purposes by the CIA. For each country there is a selection of basic economic, political and demographic information, as well as information on political or border disputes that may cause problems in the future.

Worldwide Tax (www.worldwide-tax.com*): Despite its specific-sounding name, you will find information here on a wide range of professional services, including finding local advisers, business partners and sources of capital, as well, of course, as the tax regime for both trading and selling up business assets.

BUYING YOUR COMPETITORS – THE ACQUSITION TRAIL

This is the riskiest and most costly way to increase profit, but it can also be the fastest. It will involve increasing the capital employed in your business and will add some instant turnover. You may not keep all the businesses it supplies, particularly if you are already supplying them; some businesses like to have at least two suppliers.

Buying a business has a number of advantages and disadvantages, the principal among which are as follows.

Advantages:

- Much of the uncertainty of starting up has been eliminated, so you should have fewer costly mistakes.

- You inherit relationships with customers, suppliers and perhaps even financial institutions that would otherwise take years of hard work to build.
- You may be able to pay yourself a living wage from the outset.
- You eliminate one competitor. If there are already two car-cleaning businesses in the small area in which you live, both have been around for years and yet you have decided that this is the business for you, then buying one out may make economic sense. That way you could get 50 per cent of the market rather than the third you could aim for with three players in the game.

Disadvantages:

- Valuing a private business is difficult (see Chapter 12).
- Finding a business and negotiating a purchase price can take time and may require several attempts before you succeed.
- You will need professional advice from lawyers and accountants as safeguards to ensure that you don't end up taking on hidden liabilities for tax owed, or responsibilities to past and present employees.

If you do decide to press ahead with an acquisition strategy, it's worth doing some research. Two useful ports of call are:

Acquisitions Monthly (www.aqm-e.com), which will tell you something about what deals have been done and what active sellers are in the market.
Daltons Business (www.daltonsbusiness.com), where you can see market demand statistics by different types of business.

Ikea – Growth by Acquisition

Furniture company IKEA was founded by Ingvar Kamprad when he was just 17, having cut his teeth on selling matches to his nearby neighbours at the age of 5, followed by a spell selling flower seeds, greeting cards, Christmas decorations and eventually furniture. Worth £16 billion, Kamprad is the world's seventh richest man, but his only extravagance is buying businesses. The Swedish furniture giant made eleven acquisitions over the period between 1991 and 2008, taken stakes in four companies and divested itself of six. Kamprad himself lives more frugally. He lives in a bungalow, flies easyJet and drives a 15-year-old Volvo. When he arrived at a gala dinner recently to collect a business award, he was turned away by the security guards because they saw him getting off a bus. He and his wife Margaretha are often seen dining in cheap restaurants. He does his food shopping in the afternoon when prices are lower and even then haggles prices down.

Chapter 10

Selling fivers for a tenner – why margins matter most

In terms of the skills they bring to the party, entrepreneurs are a disparate group of people. Some are natural salespeople, others born managers and strategists who prefer to leave the direct selling to partners or employees, while in this high-tech age an increasing number are technologists hawking good ideas. One talent that isn't always present is an easy familiarity with the numbers that appear on the monthly management reports or the annual accounts.

And if you run a fast-growth business, this can be a serious handicap. As sales rise, costs often escalate as well. Apparently healthy headline sales and profit figures can disguise serious problems ranging from escalating costs through to poor debtor management – issues that could bring the business down. If you want to achieve healthy and sustainable growth and improve your profit margin, it's vital to get a grip on the financials.

UNDERSTANDING THE NUMBERS

The three financial reports you need to understand are the cash-flow statement, the profit and loss account and the balance sheet. The first is simple: to project cash flow all you have to do is estimate when cash will come in and go out. For example, while you might sell to customers in January, it's quite likely to be March or even April before they pay up.

As we discussed earlier, profit is a more a matter of judgement than fact. To arrive at the profit figure you set the cash-flow assumptions aside and just measure the economic activity in the appropriate time period. So if you have sold something, whether or not you have received the cash, it goes down as income in the profit and loss account. The same goes for expense, but in this case what matters is whether it was caused by the sales in that period. Suppose that you buy in 70,000 umbrellas for £1 each, to sell for £2. If you only sell 50,000 of them in the period of the profit and loss account, then the relevant cost of stock is only £50,000.

The residue of unsold stock that cost you £20,000 will show up in the balance sheet, the home for all assets and liabilities that are not consumed in the selling process. So longer-term items such as premises and equipment appear as fixed assets. Unsold stock, work in progress, money owed by customers and cash in the bank or on hand appear as current assets in the working capital section of the balance sheet. Current liabilities such as money owed to suppliers, overdraft and unpaid tax are deducted from the current liabilities to arrive at the working capital. Adding the fixed assets to the working capital gives you the total of the money tied up in the business. So in the example below, £28,910 of capital employed is deployed to generate £8910 of net profit. This is what the figures look like.

RATIOS RULE

It's rarely much use looking at a single number in finance and expecting to glean much from it. For instance, in September 2008, after a fairly dismal few years and in the teeth of a retail recession, retailer Laura Ashley reported an increase in sales of 5.6 per cent. However, the strategy by which that growth was achieved was to open 20 new stores and the sales per store were actually down 8.8 per cent. Though the increase in sales led to profit growth of 13 per cent, profitability as measured by the amount of resource needed to generate £1 of sales had declined.

Ratios – that is, something expressed as a proportion of something else – are a better guide to what is really going on. So miles per gallon (MPG) is the ratio of fuel used per mile travelled. That's a much more useful figure than knowing that you used 20 gallons last week but have no idea how far that took you.

Ratios are used to compare performance in one period, say last month or last year, with another,this month or this year; they can also be used to see how well your business is performing compared with another, say a competitor. You can also employ ratios to compare how well you have done against your target or budget.

The ratios that matter when it comes to growing value are the six measures of profitability. Later in this chapter we will look at strategies for improving performance in these key areas:

- *Gross profit:* This is calculated by dividing the gross profit by sales and multiplying by 100. In this example the sum is $50,000/100,000 \times 100 = 50\%$. This is a measure of the value you are adding to the bought-in materials and services you need to 'make' your product or service; the higher the figure the better.

- *Operating profit:* This is calculated by dividing the oper ___ profit by sales and multiplying by 100. In this example the sum is 17,000/60,000 × 100 = 17%. This is a measure of how efficiently you are running the business, before taking account of financing costs and tax. These are excluded, as interest and tax rates change periodically and are outside your direct control. Excluding them makes it easier to compare one period with another or with another business. Once again, the rule here is the higher the figure the better. This ratio is also known as EBIT (earnings before interest and tax, earnings being the US term for profit).
- *Net profit before tax:* This is calculated by dividing the net profit before and after tax by sales and multiplying by 100. In this example the sums are 8,810/100,000 × 100 = 8.8%. This is a measure of how efficiently you are running the business after taking account of financing costs and tax.
- *Net profit after tax:* This is the profit accruing to the owners of the business after all expenses have been accounted for. The numbers here are 7,128/100,000 × 100 = 7.1%.
- *Return on capital employed (ROCE):* This is calculated by expressing the profit before interest on borrowings (finance charges) and tax as a proportion of the total capital employed. Here the numbers are 17,000/28,910 × 100 = 59%.
- *Return on shareholders' investment (ROSI):* This takes the profit after finance charges and tax as a proportion of the money the shareholders have put up. In this case the numbers are 7,128/10,210 × 100 = 70%.

If all this sounds a touch tricky, there are some useful tools that you can get help from: Biz/ed (www.bized.co.uk) and the Harvard Business School(http://harvardbusinessonline.hbsp. harvard.edu/b02/en/academic/edu_tk_acct_fin_ratio.jhtml). Both have free tools that calculate financial ratios from your financial data. They also provide useful introductions to ratio analysis, as well as defining each ratio and the formula used to calculate it. You need to register on the Harvard website to be able to download the spreadsheet.

GROWING PROFITABLE

Look back to Table 10.1. Any action that you can take that increases sales without increasing costs disproportionately will help grow either profits or profitability or both. For example, if you sell 5000 more umbrellas at £2 each you will make £5000 more gross profit. If all the other ratios hold good, your post-tax profit will rise from £7128 on sales of £100,000 to £7810 on sales of £110,000. If you can make these extra sales without any further investment in fixed assets or working capital, then the return on shareholders' funds will increase from 70 per cent to 76.5 per cent (7810/10,210).

The business, as you may already suspect and will find out why in Chapter 11, is worth more if both the amount of profit and its profitability are higher. In the last chapter we looked at the role of marketing in pushing up sales; now we can look at other ways to improve operations, efficiencies and performance and so make the business more valuable.

Improve margins

It is an unfortunate truth that over time costs tend to creep ahead of the value you are getting for the money spent. The rises happen steadily, often nearly invisibly and in increments sometimes apparently insignificant in themselves, but over time they eat away at your profit margins.

There are, however, measures you can take to improve margins.

Charge more

It is never easy raising prices, but it can, if done selectively, be a path to healthy growth. First let's examine the potential rewards and risks. Using the accounts in Table 10.1 as your working model, assume that the £100,000 of sales come from 100 shops all buying £1000 worth of umbrellas at a gross profit margin of 50 per cent. If by raising your prices by 10 per cent you lost no customers, then your profit would rise by £10,000, all of which would drop to the bottom line, before tax, as there are no additional costs involved. But what would happen if you lost five customers (5 per cent) as a result of the price rise? Now you would only have 95 customers paying

Table 10.1 Profit and loss account and balance sheet

Profit and loss account	£	Balance sheet	£	£
Sales	100,000	Fixed Assets	12,500	
– Cost of Sales	50,000			
= Gross Profit	50,000	Working capital		
– Expenses	33,000	Current Assets		
		Stock 20,000		
= Operating Profit	17,000	Debtors 3,100		
– Finance Charges	8,090	Cash 0	23,100	
		Less		
		Current Liabilities		
		Overdraft 5,000		
		Creditors 1,690		
		Tax due 0	6,690	16,410
Net Profit before tax	8,910	Capital Employed		28,910
Tax at 20%	1,782			
Net Profit after tax	7,128			
		Financed by		
		Long-term loans	18,700	
		Shareholders	10,210	
				28,910

£1100 each, so generating £104,500 of sales revenue. That's more profit than before and there are other benefits that have not been shown.

Putting the pressure on price rather than volume means carrying less stock, having fewer bills to chase, using less capital and wearing out equipment less quickly. That is not to imply that putting up prices is an easy task, but it may not be much harder than finding new customers, and it is nearly always more profitable. When raising prices try to offer some extra value in return in terms of improved service or extra features.

The above sums depend on your level of gross profit. The lower your gross profit, the less business you can afford to lose for any given price rise. A spreadsheet that does all the arithmetic of changing prices for you can be downloaded from www.innovator.com.

Use the 80/20 rule to focus on the customers that matter

In 1906, Italian economist Vilfredo Pareto used a formula to describe the unequal distribution of wealth in his country, after noting that 20 per cent of the people owned 80 per cent of the wealth. Others recognised the same relationship in their own areas of expertise, particularly quality management pioneer Dr Joseph Juran, who called the subject 'the vital few and trivial many'. Pareto's Principle is more widely known and understood as the 80/20 rule, which states that 80 per cent of effort goes into producing 20 per cent of the results. Look at Table 10.2, which is a real example showing the number of customers a salesperson had, the value of their sales and the value of their potential sales. This more or less confirms the rule, as 18 per cent of customers account for 78 per cent of sales.

Interestingly enough, when the salesperson in the company used in the above example was asked where he thought his sales

Table 10.2 The 80/20 rule in action

Number of customers		Value of sales		Value of potential sales	
	%	£000	%	£000	%
4	3	710	69	1200	71
21	18	800	78	1500	88
47	41	918	90	1600	94
116	100	1,025	100	1700	100

in two years' time would be coming from (see the last column in Table 10.2), he felt that his top 18 per cent of customers would account for 88 per cent of sales (up from 78 per cent of actual sales this year).

An analysis of this salesperson's call reports showed that over 60 per cent of time was spend calling on the bottom 68 accounts, and he planned to continue doing this. As these customers accounted for little more than 10 per cent of sales, time was being seriously misallocated. As the salesperson expected that the top 25 accounts would account for most of future growth, this misallocation of resource was scheduled to get worse. This 'activity', rather than being results based, was being used by the sales manager to make a case for an additional salesperson. What was actually needed was a call-grading system to lower the call rate on accounts with the least sales potential. For example, accounts with the least potential were called on twice a year and phoned twice, while top-grade accounts were visited up to eight times a year. When introduced the grading process saved costs, eliminated the need for an additional salesperson and freed up time so that the salesperson can prospect for new, high-potential accounts.

The 80/20 rule can be used across all areas of the business to uncover other areas where costs are being incurred that are unwarranted by the benefits. In some areas you just need to open your eyes to see waste.

Reduce the tax take

Tax on profits is often a business's biggest single expense, slicing anything from 20 to 40 per cent off the bottom line. All the money that goes in taxes can be considered a waste as far as a business is concerned. So the rule here is to minimise tax within the law. The big companies have got this down to a fine art; the top 700 UK companies paid no tax at all in 2007/8. You need to get professional advice from your accountant, but you can make a start by checking that you have charged all the allowable businesses expenses against profit using the Business Expenses Guide at www.bytstart.co.uk.

Zero-based budgets

The 80/20 rule is helpful in getting costs back into line, but what if the line was completely wrong in the first place? When you sit down with your team and discuss budgets, the arguments always revolve around how much more each section will need next year. The starting point is usually this year's costs, which are taken as the only 'facts' on which to build. For example, if you spent £25,000 on advertising last year and achieved sales of £1 million, the expense would have been 2.5 per cent of sales. If the sales budget for next year is £1.5 million, then it seems logical to spend £37,500 next year. That, however, presupposes that last year's sum was wisely and effectively spent in the first place, which it almost certainly was not.

Zero-based budgeting turns the cost argument on its head. It assumes that each year every cost centre starts from zero spending and, based on the goals of the business and the resources available, arguments are presented for every pound spent, not just for the increase proposed.

Improve your buying

There are a number of ways to reduce the cost of nearly every important business purchase. You can join an online buying group such as Buying Groups (www.buyinggroups.co.uk), Power Purchasing Group (www.ppg.co.uk) and e-Three (www.e-three.com), which help buyers to join forces and by buying in bulk get better prices and terms of trade. If you do consider buying in bulk or on longer-term contracts, make sure that the discount is high enough to compensate you for the change in trading terms.

You could also try to negotiate for better prices. Fewer than one in twenty owner-managers negotiates better deals from their suppliers. Companies such as Collective Purchasing (www.collectivepurchasing.co.uk) collect pricing information to help you negotiate without compromising on quality.

Don't leave any important area out when looking for lower costs. As well as suppliers of goods, service providers including insurance companies, utilities and banks are all well used to being negotiated with, as are accountants and lawyers. One entrepreneur talking at a Cranfield seminar outlined how he had reduced the cost of his annual audit from £7500 to £3250; his business insurance from £5500 to £4100, and the cost of invoice discounting from £14,000 to £9000.

Squeeze your capital base

Look back to Table 10.1. Suppose for one moment that it was possible to grow the profit without affecting the amount of money tied up in fixed assets. That would improve your return both on capital employed and on shareholders' investment. In fact, as long as your efforts to bump up sales don't result in a disproportionate increase in money tied up in the business, the key financial ratios that drive value will be going in the right direction.

Work hard but smarter too
The richest source of opportunities to optimise comes from finding ways to work smarter rather than harder and getting more output from a given amount of investment. Finding out about better ways to work can be difficult for a small firm where the founder has few senior employees to learn from, one of the benefits that a big business gets by virtue of continuously recruiting new people. Owner-managers can compensate for that by getting out themselves and seeing what is going on in their industry.

These are some ways you can keep abreast of the latest developments in your field:

- Read widely both the magazines that relate to your industry and those of neighbouring topics. You don't have to rush out and buy hundreds of magazines and learned journals. Use Find Articles (www.findarticles.com), which has a database of over 10 million articles on a range of topics, many of which are free and online.
- See if your competitors are doing much better than you and then try to find out why. Get their accounts from Companies House (www.companieshouse.gov.uk) and calculate some key ratios to compare performance such as those shown in biz/ed (www.bized.co.uk), and use Google News (www.google.co.uk/news) to read stories about their results and achievements in the press.

- Attend exhibitions, conferences and seminars where you are likely to meet and hear movers and shakers in your industry. Esources (www.esources.co.uk) lists trade shows, fairs and exhibitions in the UK and All Conferences.com (www.allconferences.com) is a directory focusing on conferences, conventions, trade shows, exhibitions and workshops that can be searched by category, keyword, date and venue as well as by title.

CONTROL YOUR WORKING CAPITAL

Every bit as important as the money tied up in fixed assets is the shorter-term cash revolving around the business in working capital. This is much more difficult to control than fixed assets, as decisions such as buying a new computer or a piece of machinery tend to be infrequent and considered. Letting stocks and work in progress build up and allowing customers a bit more leeway with their payments are subject to mission creep. Bit by bit as a business grows discipline slips and working capital grows, with the result that profitability declines. Having a bigger business that is less profitable is not a route to enhanced value.

Three areas to focus on in controlling working capital are:

Debtor control
If you are selling on credit and take 90 days to collect your money in from customers, which is by no means uncommon, then you are tying up an extra £150,000 cash for every £1 million of sales, compared to a firm getting its money in 35 days. For a small firm with a turnover of around £3 million a year, that could amount to the whole value of its overdraft. Or looking at it another way, getting paid a week earlier would free

up nearly £60,000 of cash and the interest that was being paid on it.

A very small amount of extra effort put in here can pay great dividends. It's important to remember that the less cash needed to finance the business, the more profitable that business will be.

Here are some things you can do to get paid faster:

- If you sell on credit, set out your terms of trade clearly on your invoices. Unless customers know when you expect to be paid, they will pay when it suits them.
- Find out when your biggest customers have their monthly cheque run and make sure your bills reach them in time.
- Send our statements promptly to chase up late payers, and always follow up with a phone call.
- Always take trade references when giving credit and look at the business's accounts to see how sound they are.

Control stock

Just-in-time production methods mean that most big businesses hold barely a few days of essential supplies. In turn, the people they buy from hold light stock levels too, which goes some way to explain why motorways and shipping lanes are busier than ever; most materials are on the move.

Small businesses tend to hold too high a level of stocks as they grow, for the simple reason that they have not yet developed a control system. You can control stock levels using a manual system of record cards with details of quantities held, who supplies you, what their delivery lead time is and at what your reorder stock level is. As you enter information on the cards you can see when it is time to take action. When you get to the point of having too many items of stock to manage manually, move up to a software solution.

Pay early, or take credit

Normally the rule is to take credit from your suppliers up to the maximum time allowed. But sometimes it may make good business sense to pay up promptly. While this may sound insane, sometimes suppliers with cash-flow difficulties of their own offer what amounts to excessively high rates of interest for settling up promptly. If a supplier offers a 2 per cent discount to pay up in 7 days rather than its usual 40 days, what is on offer is in effect 22.5 per cent equivalent interest. (Follow the steps below to work out if prompt payment is a good investment.)

So if that figure is higher than the return you are making in your own business, and your cash flow can stand the pain, paying promptly may be a better way to grow profits than any other options open in a recession. You can use the same arithmetic to work out what you can afford to pay out to get your money in earlier.

Evaluating a discount offer

1. Agree discount 2%
2. 100 – discount on offer = 98%
3. Divide step 1 by step 2 = 0.020408
4. Normal payment period in days = 40
5. Payment period to get discount = 7
6. Step 4 minus step 5 = 33
7. 365 divided by step 6 = 11.06061
8. Step 7 × step 3 × 100 = 22.572%

GETTING EXTRA HELP

As your business grows, the numbers will become more complex and the chances are that you'll need specialist help. Indeed, the decision to hire a finance director often marks the point at which a young business achieves maturity and moves to the next level. But if you have a good grasp of the figures from day one, your chances of making it to that next level will be vastly improved.

Chapter 11

Taking charge – good management's a simple yet rare commodity

You've hatched a vision, written the business plan and launched the business. Soon you will find that is the one thing you don't have is time. But crucially, a business needs as much of your time as it can get, especially in the early stages of growth. Imagine an ocean liner setting off from Europe to the US. It would have a fantastic plan, a full complement of crew, lots of great equipment on board and tanks full to bursting with fuel. But would all the preparation mean that the captain could leave the bridge unmanned and no lookouts on deck? Could he spend his whole time down in the engine room or dining with the passengers? This may sound a preposterous proposal, but that is exactly what happens in most new businesses.

By far the most important task for the founder of a super business is to plan the future strategy of that business. Most of the potential to add value to a growing business lies in shaping its future competitive strategy now and making the business better. But research by Cranfield, and others, shows that bosses spend on average only 10 per cent of their time on these tasks, preferring to spend 90 per cent on day-to-day operations. However much time bosses spend on today's business activities, they can only improve performance by a few per cent. Shaping future strategy now is where the big money lies.

And that is why it is vital to build a team. For instance, you may be a natural salesperson, but as the owner of a company your job is driving the business forward, not spending all your time on the phone in calls to clients when there are more pressing demands on your time. Nor do you want to spend your time chasing debtors. So you need to assemble a team of people who can be trusted to work hard and effectively for the good of the business. And while they handle the day-to-day tasks, you are free to build for the future.

PEOPLE PAY

In business, the simplest ratio to keep track of is sales per employee. It's a number you can calculate every day and if you have a handle on the other ratios we discussed in Chapter 9, that will serve as a reasonable proxy for profitability. As a rule of thumb, the more people you employ the more output you get per head. In fact, statistics show that firms with more than 9 and fewer than 100 employees on average generate twice the sales per head as those employing fewer than 9. Those employing between 100 and 499 produce three times the sales per head of the smallest businesses, although then the efficiencies start to drop off. The reasons for such gains are not too difficult to appreciate. All a business's fixed costs, premises, equipment, website set-up and so forth can be better utilised by more employees. People can also be employed to do what they do best, rather than having to be jacks of all trades.

Adam Smith on the power of organised production

The greatest improvement in the productive powers of labour, and the greater part of the skill, dexterity, and judgment with which it is anywhere directed, or applied, seem to have been the effects of the division of labour ... I have seen a small manufactory of this kind where ten men only were employed, and where some of them consequently performed two or three distinct operations. But though they were very poor, and therefore but indifferently accommodated with the necessary machinery, they could, when they exerted themselves, make among them about twelve pounds of pins in a day. There are in a pound upwards of four thousand pins of a middling size. Those ten persons, therefore, could make among them upwards of forty-eight thousand pins in a day. But if they had all wrought separately and independently, and without any of them having been educated to this peculiar business, they certainly could not each of them have made twenty.

By Smith's calculations, organising production efficiently increased output by 2400 times, leaving the market itself as the primary limiting factor.

Source: Adam Smith , *An Inquiry into the Nature and Causes of the Wealth of Nations*, 1776.

MAXIMISING EMPLOYEE PERFORMANCE

You will remember from Chapter 4 that averages can be tricky concepts, but the one certainty is that some growing businesses are less successful than the average and some much better. This would have been no surprise to Douglas McGregor, a founding faculty member of MIT's Sloan School of Management. He began his management classic *The Human Side of Enterprise* by asking: 'What are your assumptions about the most effective way to manage people?' This seemingly simple question led to a fundamental revolution in management thinking. McGregor went on to claim, 'The effectiveness of organisations could be at least doubled if managers could discover how to tap into the unrealised potential present in their workforces.'

But employees are not a trouble-free resource. To maximise employee performance ratios, you have to manage your employees so that they produce quality work for you. You have to build them into teams, and lead and manage them to prepare them for the roller-coaster life of change that is the inevitable lot of a small, growing business. Finding the right people, keeping them on side, motivating, managing and rewarding them are the defining distinctions between the most successful organisations and the mediocre.

Good management is also the key to maximising a business's value, both as it grows and on exit. In order to create value the founder needs the time and space to develop and implement growth strategies. For a founder to exit a business either wholly or partially, that business has to be demonstrably capable of surviving and prospering without him or her. In either case this requires building a team capable of running the business and taking it on to the next stage.

RECRUITMENT – FINDING THE RIGHT STAFF

Taking on new employees is often a more expensive exercise than buying a major item of machinery or a heavy goods vehicle. If that sounds improbable just check out the figures: the advertising for a middle-ranking executive on a salary of £40,000 may well cost £6000. If the employee is taken on using a recruitment consultant you can expect a bill of around a fifth of the first year's pay (£8000). Three days interviewing, testing, preparing a contract of employment, perhaps paying a share of the new 'removal expenses' will bring the total bill up to around £20,000. If you get the wrong candidate, and there is a good chance of that happening if you fail with any element of the recruitment process, then you may have to double that figure. Then of course there is the cost of not getting the job done that you were recruiting for in the first place.

Staffing problems can cost you business

Roger had worked for a large national firm of builder's merchants for ten years before he branched out on his own. He had trained as a plumber, so he was confident that he would have no difficulty in finding work, and he was right. Soon Roger was working a 60-hour week, returning home exhausted late in the evening to do his paperwork and plan for the next day's work. Within four months of starting up Roger desperately needed more staff. An acquaintance recommended an out-of-work plumber who could work for Roger almost immediately. Roger reckoned that anyone was better than no one, as at least some of the backlog of work could be tackled. He took the man on and sent his new employee to work on a small task for a customer. The task should have taken three days and Roger planned to try and get out to see how he was getting on during the first day. Unfortunately Roger couldn't get out to that job until the afternoon of the second day. He arrived to find that his new workman had failed to show up for work that day and had produced such a

> low standard of work that everything had to be done
> again. Roger ended up losing a valued client, wasting
> valuable materials, and still had the job to do at a later
> date.

There are plenty of ways to find employees; for finding the *right* employees the choices are more limited. Research at Cranfield revealed some important statistics. First, nearly two thirds of all first appointments fail, with employees leaving in weeks or months having contributed little or nothing save some extra cost and pain. Secondly, there were marked differences in the success rate that appear to be dependent on the sources used to find employees. These are the main options ranked in order of likelihood of making a successful appointment:

- *Employing an agency or consultant:* This is the least popular, most expensive and most successful recruitment method. Only one in fifteen small firms does this for its early appointments, but when it does it is three times more likely to get the right person. The reasons for success are in part the value added by the agency or consultant in helping get the job description and pay package right; and the fact that they have already pre-interviewed prospective employees before they put them forward.
- *Tapping into the family:* Employing family members has a number of key advantages. First, they are a known quantity and you can usually vouch for their honesty and reliability. In the second place you can ask them to work on conditions and for hours that would be neither acceptable nor legally allowed for any other employee. Against that, you need to weigh up the difficulties you may have if they can't do the work to the standard or in the manner you like and you have to dispense with their services.

- *Advertising in the press:* Local papers are good for generally available skills and where the pay is such that people expect to live close to where they work. National papers are much more expensive to advertise in but attract a wider pool of people with a cross-section of skills, including those not necessarily available locally. Trade and specialist papers and magazines are useful if it is essential that your applicant has a specific qualification, say in accountancy or computing. The goal of a job advertisement is not just to generate responses from suitably qualified applicants, but also to screen out applicants who are clearly unqualified. If you make the job sound more attractive than it really is and are too vague about the sort of person you are looking for, you could end up with hundreds of applicants. Lara Morgan's Pacific Direct puts its advertisements sideways on, so that applicants have to turn the paper round to read them. They claim this lets people see they want people who look at things in unconventional ways to apply and that they are not a run-of-the-mill firm that works like any other.

- *Using the Internet:* Nearly a quarter of all jobs are filled using job boards, websites where employees and employers can get together much along the lines of a dating agency. The Internet's advantages are speed, cost and reach. You can get your job offer in front of thousands of candidates in seconds. The fees are usually modest, often less than regional paper job adverts. Services through job boards range from passive, where employers and employees just find each other, to proactive, where online candidate databases are searched and suitable candidates are made aware of your vacancy. The latter, unsurprisingly, has a higher success rate.

- *Using your network:* Nearly two out of every three very small businesses use business contacts and networks when they are recruiting. This route is favoured because it is cheap, informal and can be pursued without the bother of writing a job

171

description. The job can then in effect be infinitely varied to suit the candidates that may surface. Unfortunately, the statistics indicate that two out of five appointments made through personal contacts fail within six months and the business is back in the recruiting game again. The reason for failure lies in the absence of rigour that the approach encourages; only if you can take a thorough approach and be sure of a genuine reason for someone wanting to recommend a person to you should you recruit in this way.

Testing for the best – getting the selection process right

What are known as the classic trio of selection methods – application forms, interviews and references – can be supplemented by other tools that can improve your chances of getting the right candidate for most of the jobs you may want to fill. These tools are often clustered under the general heading of psychometric tests, although most of the tests themselves have less to do with psychology than with basic aptitude.

Tests are particularly useful for small firms as they can provide a much needed and valuable external view on candidates, which big firms have already in their human resources departments. Tests can also be applied quickly and without using many scarce internal resources.

Used correctly, fairly and in the right situations, tests can objectively measure skills (such as word processing or software proficiency), assess acquired knowledge and qualifications and determine aptitude for certain jobs. But although tests are popular and becoming more reliable, they are neither certain to get selection decisions right nor risk free.

There are dozens of commercial test publishers producing over 3000 different tests. You can locate the appropriate test for your business through the British Psychological Society (www.bps.org.uk), The Work Foundation (www.theworkfoundation.com) or the Chartered Institute of Personnel and Development (www.cipd.co.uk).

THE IMPORTANCE OF TEAMWORK

Teams are a powerful way to get superb results out of even the most average individual employees. With effective teamwork, a small firm can raise its efficiency levels to world-class standards. Some small firms have built their entire success around teams.

A group of people working together is not necessarily a team, however. A successful sports team will have the right number of players for the game, each with a clearly defined role. There will be a coach, to train and improve players' performances, and there will be measurable goals to achieve in the shape of obvious competitors to beat. Contrast that with the situation that usually prevails in a typical small firm. The number of players is the number who turn up on a particular day, and few have specific roles to play. Some are trained and properly equipped and some are not. For the most part the business's objectives are not clearly explained to employees, nor are any performance-measuring tools disclosed. It is highly likely that most of the players in the home team do not even know the name or characteristics of the enemy against which they are competing.

Clearly, a successful sports team and an unorganised group of co-workers have little in common, but what needs to be done to weld people at work into a team is also clearly visible.

Teams don't just happen. However neat the CVs and convincing the organisational chart, you can't just turn out a team-in-a-box. The presumption that people are naturally going to work together is usually a mistake. Chaos is more likely than teamwork.

Successful teams have certain features in common. They all have strong and effective leadership; clear objectives; appropriate resources; the ability to communicate freely throughout the organisation; the authority to act quickly on decisions; a good balance of team members, with complementary skills and talents; the ability to work collectively; and a size appropriate to the task.

Anatomy of a balanced team

Experts in team behaviour such as R. Meredith Belbin (www.belbin.com) have identified the key team profiles that are essential if a team is to function well. Any one person may perform more than one of these roles. The key roles are:

- *Chairperson/team leader:* Stable, dominant, extrovert. Concentrates on objectives. Does not originate ideas. Focuses people on what they do best.
- *Plant:* Dominant, high IQ, introvert. A 'scatterer of seeds' who originates ideas. Misses out on detail. Thrustful but easily offended.
- *Resource investigator:* Stable, dominant, extrovert and sociable. Lots of contacts with the outside world. Strong on networks. Salesperson/diplomat/liaison officer. Not an original thinker.
- *Shaper:* Anxious, dominant, extrovert. Emotional and impulsive. Quick to challenge and to respond to a challenge. Unites ideas, objectives and possibilities. Competitive. Intolerant of woollyness and vagueness.

- *Company worker:* Stable, controlled. A practical organiser. Can be inflexible but likely to adapt to established systems. Not an innovator.
- *Monitor evaluator:* High IQ, stable, introvert. Goes in for measured analysis not innovation. Unambiguous and often lacking enthusiasm, but solid and dependable.
- *Team worker:* Stable, extrovert, but not really dominant. Much concerned with individual's needs. Builds on others' ideas. Cools things down when tempers fray.
- *Finisher:* Anxious introvert. Worries over what could go wrong. Permanent sense of urgency. Preoccupied with order. Concerned with 'following through'.

Reproduced with kind permission of Belbin Associates (www.belbin.com)

MOTIVATING? JUST AVOID DEMOTIVATING

In order to have a team of employees who work well for you, you need to motivate them – but how do you do that?

The first hint in the business world that there might be more to motivation than rewards and redundancy came with Harvard Business School professor Elton Mayo's renowned Hawthorne Studies. These were conducted between 1927 and 1932 at the Western Electric Hawthorne Works in Chicago. Starting out to see what effect illumination had on productivity, Mayo moved on to see how fatigue and monotony fitted into the equation by varying rest breaks, temperature, humidity and work hours, even providing a free meal at one point. Working with a team of six women, Mayo changed every parameter he could think of, including increasing and decreasing working hours and rest breaks, and finally he returned to the original conditions. Every change resulted in an improvement in productivity, except when two ten-minute pauses morning and afternoon were expanded to six five-minute pauses. These frequent work pauses, the women felt, upset their work rhythm. Mayo's conclusion was that 'showing someone upstairs cares', engendering a sense of ownership and responsibility were important motivators that could be harnessed by management.

Another American, Douglas McGregor, formalised management thinking on motivation into two dominant schools of thought. Under Theory X, the belief is that the average person has an inherent dislike of work and will avoid it if possible. So management needs to put emphasis on productivity, incentive schemes and the idea of a 'fair day's work'. Theory Y concludes that under the right conditions hard work can be source of great satisfaction, that personal recognition is the highest 'reward' that can be given and that it will result in the greatest level of commitment to the task in hand.

The next piece in the motivational jigsaw was provided by Frederick Herzberg, professor of psychology at Case Western Reserve University in Cleveland, who discovered that distinctly separate factors were the cause of job satisfaction and dissatisfaction (see Table 11.1). The first group he called motivators, covering areas such as achievement, recognition, responsibility, advancement and job interest. The second he called hygiene factors and these causes of job dissatisfaction include company policy, supervision, salary, working conditions and interpersonal relationships. He reasoned that a lack of hygiene will cause disease, but the presence of hygienic conditions will not, of itself, produce good health. So the lack of adequate 'job hygiene' will cause dissatisfaction, but hygienic conditions alone will not bring about job satisfaction; to do that you have to work on the determinants of job satisfaction.

Table 11.1 Motivators and hygiene

Motivators	Hygiene factors
• *Achievement.* People want to succeed, so if you can set goals that people can reach and better they will be much more satisfied than if they are constantly missing targets. • *Recognition.* Everyone likes their hard work to be acknowledged. Not everyone wants that recognition made in the same way, however. • *Responsibility.* People like the opportunity to take responsibility for their own work and for the whole task. This helps them grow as individuals. • *Advancement.* Promotion or at any rate progress are key motivators. In a small firm providing career prospects for key staff can be a fundamental reason for growth. • *Attractiveness of working itself.* (job interest) There is no reason a job should be dull. You need to make people's jobs interesting and give them a say in how their work is done. That will encourage new ideas on how things can be done better.	• *Company policy.* Rules, formal and informal, such as start and finish times, meal breaks, dress code. • *Supervision.* The extent to which employees are allowed to get on with the job, or whether they have someone looking over their shoulders all day. • *Administration.* Whether things work well, or paperwork is in a muddle and supplies always come in late. • *Salary.* Whether employees are getting at least the going rate and benefits comparable with others. • *Working conditions.* Whether people are expected to work in substandard conditions with poor equipment and little job security. • *Interpersonal relationship.* Whether the atmosphere at work is good or people are at daggers drawn.

Source: Based on Frederick Herzberg, 'One more time: How do you motivate employees?', Harvard Business Review, *Jan/Feb 1968.*

RELEVANT REWARDS

So rewards are one aspect of motivation. While people often come to work for a set number of hours each week, it is what they do during that time that matters most to the organisation. Deciding arbitrarily the pay rates of people who work for you may appear to be one of the perks of working for yourself. But inconsistent pay rates will quickly upset people and staff will jump ship at the first opportunity. How much is the right amount? Get it too low and your ability to attract and retain productive and reliable people capable of growing as your business grows is impaired. But pay too much and your overheads rise so much you become uncompetitive. That is a real danger for small firms, where the wages bill often represents the largest single business expense.

These ground rules are not very complicated but they are important:

- Only pay what you can afford. There is no point in sinking the company with a wage bill that it can't meet.
- Make sure that pay is fair and equitable and is seen as such by everyone.
- Make sure that people know how pay scales are arrived at.
- See that pay scales for different jobs reflect the relative importance of the job and the skills required.
- Ensure that your pay scales are in line with the law on minimum wage requirements and are competitive with those of other employers in your region or industry.

There are also important ground rules for matching pay to performance:

- Make the rules clear so everyone knows how the reward system will work.

- Make the goals specific and if possible quantifiable.
- Make the reward visible so everyone knows what each person or team gets.
- Make it matter – the reward has to be worthwhile and commensurate with the effort involved.
- Make it fair, so that people believe their reward is correctly calculated.
- Make it realistic, because if the target is set too high no one will try to achieve it.
- Make it happen quickly.

Different strokes – tailoring rewards

You also should recognise that different types of work have different measurable outcomes. Those outcomes have to be identified and a scale arrived at showing the base rate of pay and payment above that base for achieving objectives, making sure that you pick the right mix of goals and rewards. The most common results-based reward systems include:

- *Paying a commission:* This is perhaps the easiest reward system, but it really only works for those directly involved in selling. A commission is a payment based in some way on the value of sales secured by the individual or team concerned. It makes sense to base the commission on your gross profit rather than sales turnover, otherwise you could end up rewarding salespeople for generating unprofitable business.
- *Awarding bonuses:* In general, bonuses are tied to total business results and though it's less obvious how an individual contributed directly to the result achieved, bonuses can be motivational for team work.
- *Sharing profits:* This involves giving a specific share of the company's profit to employees. The share of the profits can

be different for different jobs, length of service or seniority. This type of reward has the great merit of focusing everyone's attention on the firm's primary economic goal – to make money. If profits go up, people get more; but the result can go the other way too, which can be less attractive. Also, profit targets can be missed for reasons outside employees' direct control. However unfair this may seem, it is the hard reality of business. If you think your employees are adult enough to take that fact on board, then this can be a useful way to reward staff.

- *Sharing ownership:* These schemes give employees the chance to share in the increase in value of a company's shares, giving them a long-term stake in the business. Hopefully it will make them look beyond short-term issues and ensure their long-term loyalty.

DELEGATE, DON'T DUMP

Overwork is a common complaint of those running their own business and a prime reason for recruiting staff. There is never enough time to think or plan, but if you don't make time to plan you will never grow a valuable business. Delegating some tasks would ease the stress.

However, many owner-managers are unable to delegate, either because they draw comfort from sticking to routine tasks such as sending out invoices, rather than tackling new and unfamiliar ones such as keeping up on developments in the industry, or because they just don't know how to delegate. Either way, neither the business nor those in it can grow until delegation becomes the normal way to operate.

Delegation is a management process not to be confused with 'dumping', in which unpopular, difficult or tedious tasks are unceremoniously shoved onto the shoulders of the first person who comes to hand. Delegation is the art of getting things done your way by other people. Or as one entrepreneur succinctly put it, 'making other people happy to make you rich'. Delegation probably won't save the boss any time. All it will do is let them spend the time they want to dedicate to work more productively, profitably and enjoyably.

Delegating, in common with many first attempts in management, often fails. Learning how to delegate effectively takes time and practice. It won't happen overnight, but if it doesn't happen the business will never realise its potential. Delegating brings benefits to everyone involved in the process.

Benefits for the boss include:

- More time to achieve more today and to plan for the future. In this way time can be freed up to tackle high value-added tasks such as recruitment and selection, or motivation.
- Back-up for emergencies and day-to-day tasks. If you can delegate successfully, you have a reserve of skilled people who can keep the business running profitably if you're not there. This can also give customers and financial backers the comfort of knowing that they are not dealing with a one-man band whose operation would fall apart without him or her.

Benefits for employees include:

- The opportunity to develop new skills. Failing to delegate deprives employees of the opportunity to learn new skills and to grow themselves, and drives good employees, just the ones a growing organisation desperately needs, away for greater challenges. Employees who have assumed the responsibility for new tasks train their staff in the same way.

Then the organisation can grow and have management in depth.

- Greater involvement. Research consistently shows that employees rank job satisfaction as of equal or greater value than pay in their working life. Delegation encourages people to take ownership of their decisions and will increase their enthusiasm and initiative for their work, and so get more satisfaction from it.

Benefits for the business are:

- Efficiency improves, by allowing those closest to the problems and issues being faced to take the decisions in a timely manner.
- Flexibility of operations increases. Because several people are able to perform key tasks, they can be rotated and expanded or contracted to meet changing circumstances. Delegation also results in more people being prepared for promotion.

Delegating successfully – a five-point plan

1. *Decide what to delegate:* Tasks that are less easy to delegate include all confidential work, discipline, staff evaluation, complex or sensitive issues and strategic matters that can only be decided by the boss. Anything else that saves you a reasonable amount of time is in the frame. Delegation itself is a form of risk taking, so if you can't deal with a few mistakes delegation will prove difficult.

2. *Decide whom to delegate to:* The factors to consider here include who has the necessary skills or could be trained up? Whose workload will allow them to take

---

on the task and are they likely to be or continue to be a loyal employee?

3. *Communicate your decision:* Discuss the task you propose to delegate one to one with the individual concerned. Confirm that they feel up to the task or agree any necessary training, back-up or extra resources. Set out clearly in writing the task broken down into its main components, the measurable outcomes, the timescales and any other important factors. Then let others in the business know of your decision.

4. *Manage and evaluate:* From the outset, establish set times to meet with the person delegated to and review their performance. Make the time intervals between these reviews short at first, lengthening the period when their performance is satisfactory. The secret of successful delegation is to follow up.

5. *Reward the result:* Things that get measured get done and those that are rewarded get done over again. The reward need not be financial. Recognition or praise for a job well done are often more valuable to an ambitious person than money.

WELCOME CHANGE

The late professor Peter Drucker claimed that the first task of a leader is to define the company's mission. In a world in which product and service life cycles are shrinking, new technologies have an ever-shorter shelf life and customers demand ever higher levels of both quality and innovation, entrepreneurial leadership means inspiring change and adapting the business to an increasingly volatile and competitive environment. Small firms are usually better at handling change than big firms, but they rarely set the agenda. That's down either to big firms, which usually define the standards in an industry so that the small firms have to scramble to keep up; or to turbulence in the economy, which can sink small firms unless they can adapt and change quickly.

However, recognising the need for change falls a long way short of being able to implement it successfully. Few people like change and even fewer can adapt to new circumstances quickly and without missing a heartbeat.

Change is normal and a management process just like any other

By definition, a small business seeking growth must be able to manage a fast rate of change. Entrepreneurs must see change as the norm and not as a temporary and unexpected disruption, which will go away when things improve.

Because change is inevitable and unpredictable in its consequences doesn't mean that it can't be managed as a process. These are the stages in managing change:

- *Tell them why:* Change is better accepted when people are given a compelling business reason. Few bankers would question the need for change after the 2008 debacles at Bear Stearns, SocGen, Northern Rock *et al.*
- *Make it manageable:* Even when people accept what needs to be done, the change may just be too big for anyone to handle. Breaking it down into manageable bits can help it be overcome.
- *Take a shared approach:* Involve people early on, asking them to join you in managing change and giving key participants some say in shaping the change right from the start. This will reduce the feeling that change is being imposed and more brains will be brought to bear on the problem.

- *Reward success early:* Flag up successes as quickly as possible. Don't wait for the year end or the appraisal cycle. This will inspire confidence and keep the change process on track.
- *Expect resistance:* You can be reasonably certain that not everyone will welcome every change, however self-evident and essential it is. So anticipate resistance, assess where it will come from and plan to overcome it.
- *Recognise that change takes longer than expected:* People go through six stages when experiencing change and hence the reason the process takes so long. The stages are immobilisation or shock, disbelief, depression, acceptance of reality, testing out the new situation, rationalising why it is happening and then finally acceptance. Most major changes make things worse before they make them better. More often than not, the immediate impact of change is a decrease in productivity as people struggle to cope with new ways of working and move up their own learning curve. The doubters will gloat and even the change champions may waver. But the greatest danger then is pulling the plug on the plan and either adopting a new plan or reverting to the status quo. To prevent this disappointment it is vital both to set realistic goals for the change period, and to anticipate the time lag between change and results.

Change works – motivating through consensual management

John Huggett, a young and abrasive entrepreneur, moved south from Yorkshire and bought a small but seriously troubled engineering factory. The company then employed 22 people and had shrunk over the years from more than 50. The business had suffered losses for over a year. Nevertheless, Huggett succeeded brilliantly in solving the problems that had built up over time.

In the process, by his own admission he came close to committing murder as telephone directories and occasionally the telephone itself flew through the air. John was perceived, not unnaturally given his style and the rescue job he was attempting, as a fire-eating monster. No one saw the human behind the gruff exterior.

At that time it didn't matter. However, as the factory moved into a period of growth and expansion, John recognised that he and the management team needed to make a conscious effort to change towards a more consensual style of management. People didn't feel empowered and they weren't about to stick their necks out when the blood still ran from the walls. John stood up in front of the workforce and said, 'We are going to have a different management style, and we are going to change.' He introduced an attitude survey to take the temperature of the water and committed himself, in advance of the survey, to live by its results.

This he and the management team have done, introducing exceptionally effective team briefings, management walkabouts and other consultative mechanisms. It took time for the workforce to be convinced, but they came to greatly respect John's integrity and open style.

MOVING ON

Managing effectively and building an effective team will help you create a successful, dynamic and expanding company, but it will do something else as well. When you come to sell, the business will be a much more valuable proposition if buyers can see that in addition to the founder/owner there is a strong management and a motivated workforce. Indeed, buyers will be reassured by the knowledge that when the owner cashes in and moves on, those who remain will be more than capable of taking the company forward.

GET
BOUGHT

Chapter 12

What's it to you?
Calculating value

You can do very well out of running a business. Whether you pay yourself a salary, dividends or a mixture of the two, a healthy and profitable business provides a good income. But in most cases the income generated by a business won't make you rich. The serious money is released when the time comes to sell up.

And the chances are there will come a time when you want to sell all or part of the business. It may be simply that you feel the time is right to cash in and reap the rewards of all your hard work. The promise of a yacht and a world trip can be a powerful motivator. That said, not everyone looks forward to a life of leisure. For the so-called serial entrepreneur, the sale of one business is often the cue to either start another or seek third-party investment opportunities. And sometimes the trigger is the realisation that you have taken the company as far as you can and the time is right to let someone else take over.

It has to be said that the decision may not be entirely down to the founder. When venture capital investors come on board, they inevitably work towards an exit – generally through a sale or flotation – that will allow them to realise their investment. This is often the point where the founder also bows out.

But whatever the reason, the sale of a business is your opportunity to enjoy some serious money. It could also be a once-in-a-lifetime opportunity, so it's important that you get the best deal possible. The first step is to take a long, hard look at what your business is worth.

That isn't always straightforward. The value of a business is, quite simply, what a third party will pay, so any valuation prior to a deal is to a greater or lesser extent notional. However, there are some tried-and-tested measures that will provide you with a pretty good idea of the kind of sum you can expect to achieve.

PRICE/EARNINGS RATIO

The simplest and most usual way for businesses to be valued is using a formula known as the price/earnings ratio. The P/E ratio is calculated by dividing the share price into the amount of profit earned for each share. For example, if a business makes £100,000 profit and has 1000 shares, the profit per share is £100. If the share price of that company is £10, then its P/E ratio is 10 (100/10). So much for the science, now for the art: P/E ratios vary both with the business sector and current market sentiment for that sector.

For example, the high-tech sector may have a P/E ratio of 30 or more: Google had a P/E of 100 at one point. That means that shareholders were prepared to pay £100 for every £1 of profit the company was making. For Barclays Bank, however, they were only paying £10 for every £1 of profits and in the market mayhem of 2008 the banking sector slipped well below that. The market as a whole trades with P/Es of between 10 and 20.

You can check out the P/E for your business sector either by looking in the *Financial Times*, or if you can't wait until morning check out the performance tables on ProShare's website (www. proshareclubs.co.uk). There you can see the current P/E ratio for every company in your sector, as long as they are listed on the London Stock Exchange. If you want to see how much interest there is in your business sector right now, visit Interactive Investor (www.iii.co.uk). There you can see the sector whose shares have been bought and sold the most over the past day, month and year.

However, private companies don't trade on as high a P/E multiple as their big brothers on the stock market. So if a public company in your sector is on a P/E of 12, as a private company your prospective P/E would be around 8, or a third less. Why? Good question. The simplest answer is that while shares in your business are hard to dispose of, you can unload shares in a public company every business day by making a phone call to your broker. In other words, the premium is for liquidity.

BDO Stoy Hayward's Private Company Price Index (PCPI) tracks the relationship between the current FTSE price/earnings ratio and the P/Es currently being paid on the sale of private companies. Put simply, the PCPI lets a company without a stock market listing get a reasonable idea of what it will actually sell for now (www.bdo.co.uk).

DISCOUNTING FUTURE EARNINGS

A valuation technique popular with the venture capital community is to discount future earnings. We know intuitively that getting cash in sooner is better than getting it in later. In other words, a pound received now is worth more than a pound that will arrive in one, two or more years in the future because of what we could do with that money ourselves, or because of what we ourselves have to pay out to have use of that money. So anyone buying your business will need to ascribe a value to a future stream of earnings to arrive at what is known as the present value. If we know we could earn 20 per cent on any money, we then know the maximum we would be prepared to pay now for 1 coming in one year hence would be around 80p. If we were to pay 1 now to get 1 back in a year's time, we would in effect be losing money.

The process used to handle this is known as discounting and the technique is termed discounted cash flow (DCF). The residual discounted cash is called the net present value.

The first column in Table 12.1 shows the simple cash-flow implications of an investment proposition: a surplus of £5000 comes after five years from putting £20,000 into a project. But if we accept the proposition that future cash is worth less than current cash, the only question we need to answer is how much

Table 12.1 Discounting a stream of future earnings

£	Cash flow A	Discount factor at 15% B	Discounted cash flow A × B
Initial cash cost now (Year 0)	20,000	1.00	20,000
Net cash flows			
Year 1	1,000	0.8695	870
Year 2	4,000	0.7561	3,024
Year 3	8,000	0.6575	5,260
Year 4	7,000	0.5717	4,002
Year 5	5,000	0.4972	2,486
Total	25,000	15,642	
Cash surplus	5,000	Net Present Value	(4,358)

less. If we assume that an investor wants to make at least a 15 per cent return on their investment, then that is the discount rate selected (this doesn't matter too much, as you will see in the section on internal rate of return).

The formula for calculating what a pound received at some future date is:

$$\text{Present value}(PV) = £P \times 1/(1 + r)n$$

where £P is the initial cash cost, r is the interest rate expressed in decimals and n is the year in which the cash will arrive.

So if we decide on a discount rate of 15 per cent, the present value of £1 received in one year's time is:

Present value = $£1 \times 1/(1 + 0.15)1 = 0.87$ (rounded to two decimal places).

So we can see that our £1000 arriving at the end of year one has a present value of £870; the £4000 in year two has a present value of £3024; and by year five present value reduces cash flows to barely half their original figure. In fact, far from having a real payback in year four and generating a cash surplus of £5000, this project will make us £4358 worse off than we had hoped to be if we required to make a return of 15 per cent. The investment in buying this business fails to meet the criteria using DCF.

INTERNAL RATE OF RETURN (IRR)

DCF is a useful starting point, but it does not give us any definitive information. For example, all we know about the above investment is that it doesn't make a return of 15 per cent. In order to know the actual rate of return, we need to choose a discount rate that produces a net present value of the entire cash flow of zero, known as the internal rate of return.

The maths is time consuming, but Solution Matrix website (www.solutionmatrix.com) has a tool for working out payback, discounted cash flow, internal rate of return and a whole lot more calculations relating to capital budgeting. You have to register on the site first before downloading its free capital budgeting spreadsheet suite and tutorial. From the home page you should click on 'Download Center' and 'Download Financial Metrics Lite for Microsoft Excel'.

Using this spreadsheet, you will see that the IRR for the project in question is slightly under 7 per cent, not much better than bank interest and certainly insufficient to warrant taking any risks for. Venture capital providers will be looking for an IRR of above 30 per cent.

RULES OF THUMB

Some business sectors have their own yardsticks for estimating the value of a business. For example, sales turnover is often used for computer maintenance or mail-order businesses; the number of customers for a mobile phone airtime provider; the number of outlets for an estate agency, restaurant or pub chain; and grocery shops are valued partly on their turnover and partly on the value of the stock they hold. BizStats (www.bizstats.com) has a nifty table giving a list of these rules.

City Flyer Express – a rule-of-value based on landing slots

Robert Wright, who started up his venture, Connectair, immediately after completing his MBA at Cranfield, sold out to Harry Goodman, late of International

Leisure fame, for around £7 million. Not bad for just under five years' work. However, negotiations with Goodman took up nearly a year and the opening offer was under £1 million. In the end the deal was valued on a multiple of landing slots, as Goodman planned to use these for his fleet of much larger planes and so create value.

Things didn't quite work out as planned and International Leisure went bust. Robert bought the business back from receivership for a nominal £1 and with £1 million of venture capital from 3i built the business up again, this time under the name City Flyer Express. A decade later he sold the business to British Airways for a healthy £75 million.

MULTIPLE MODELS

Some valuation techniques, particularly those used by business brokers who help sell private companies, involve using a number of adjustments to the basic P/E method. One such approach is based around the following formula:

Add-back profitability × Industry sector P/E + Adjustment for assets and liabilities

The add-back profitability involves trying to arrive at what the profit might be in the hands of the acquiring company. In the case where the reported profit of a business for sale is £500,000, it might be argued that the £50,000 of interest charges should be added back to the profits based on the fact that new owners would finance the company in a different way and would have access to these funds as disposable profits. The same argument could be made for the two directors who are paying themselves a hefty £300,000 a year, when in fact the business could be run with a divisional manager by the acquirer paying around £100,000, including a performance-related bonus. That would add a further £200,000 to the profits being available in the business. There could be deductions to profits too, if the acquiring firm doesn't expect to be able to retain the income stream post purchase: specialist consultancy income from work done by one of the owners or the rental income arising from letting out part of the business premises if that won't continue, for example. To carry on our example, let's assume that amounts to a deduction of £100,000. So the business's continuing profits would be assessed as:

$$£500,000 + £50,000 + £200,000 - £100,000 = £650,000$$

That figure would then be the basis from which to apply the P/E multiple. In the case where the sector P/E is 5, then the value would be £3.25 million rather than the £2.5 million that would otherwise have been assumed.

There is one further adjustment made in this valuation approach: an adjustment for assets and liabilities is made by calculating the net assets; that is, the surplus of assets over liabilities. The argument for this is that this represents the current value of the owners' stake in the business. The P/E approach gives the value of future earnings. So adding one to the other gives the 'real' value. In practice, any valuation approach is just the starting point for negotiations.

VALUING MINORITY SHAREHOLDINGS

If there are several shareholders, the chances are that one or more will have smaller stakes than the business founder. The value of their stake will not just be smaller because they have fewer shares, but by virtue of the fact that a minority stake usually can neither force nor prevent the sale of a business. Discounts are applied to most share calculations for a lack of marketability.

The HM Revenue & Customs website is useful for understanding this area and information can be found in the manuals section at www.hmrc.gov.uk. It describes some ideas of how to value 50 per cent of a company. Further guidance on values greater than 50 per cent can be found at www.hmrc.gov.uk/manuals/svmanual/svm06120.htm.

Once the shareholding drops below 50 per cent details are less precise. The website does not give any details regarding minority shareholders and does not suggest that the discount should be greater in this instance.

EASY VALUE CALCULATIONS

There are three special situations that make valuation relatively easy. They are:

- *Public companies:* If your business is already floated on a stock market its value is measured by buyers and sellers every day, or perhaps more often in turbulent times. For example, during the banking meltdown in the autumn of 2008 HBOS's shares oscillated by as much as 40 per cent on an almost daily basis. It was not alone in seeing violent swings and indeed some stock markets, most prominently the Russian main market, actually had to shut down as both the volume of selling orders and the spread of prices were too great to comprehend, yet alone manage. Nevertheless, the market sets the value of every business on a stock exchange for every transaction. This market price is not necessarily the price that the owners will get for their shares, but in more normal times it is a reasonably close approximation.

- *Asset sale:* Ongoing businesses are valued by some measure of future expected profits. In fact, the accounts don't even attempt to put a value on the assets. Fixed assets, except for freehold property, are recorded at the cost at date of purchase, reduced by a notional depreciation amount, the sole purpose of which is to allocate costs over an asset's working life. The asset itself could be of virtually no value at all, such as secondhand office furniture, but that would not be revealed in the balance sheet, whose purpose in this respect is only to show where money has come from and what has been done with that money. The exception to this rule is if a business is not going to continue trading, for example if no buyer can be found. In those circumstances the assets now all have to be valued and sold off piecemeal.
- *Failures:* It is an unfortunate fact of business life that over 400,000 businesses close down each year in the UK alone. Certainly not all are financial disasters and it may still be possible to extract some value from selling off the assets; if anything is left over after all liabilities have been met the owners may get a very modest payout. The best options are to try and steer the business into what is known as a voluntary arrangement with your creditors. A creditors' meeting can be called notifying all creditors of your plan to meet liabilities and if the proposal is approved by more than 75 per cent by value of the creditors' meeting, it will be binding on all creditors. Then you can have another shot at creating value. Don't be too daunted, as plenty of great entrepreneurs have had a bumpy time with their initial ventures.

BE PREPARED TO NEGOTIATE

Ultimately, you won't know what your business is worth until you sit down around a table with potential buyers and hammer out a deal. The above formulae can give you a pretty good idea, and by working with an experienced mergers and acquisitions adviser you can factor in the impact of current market conditions on price, but you can never be sure what a buyer will be prepared to pay. You can, however, be certain of what you are prepared to accept. That kind of certainty will help you hold your own during negotiations.

Equally importantly, you should also be aware that there are a great many steps that you can take to optimise and maximise the value of your business. That's what we'll be looking at in the next chapter.

Chapter 13

Dressing to kill – preparing your business for sale and getting the timing right

Everyone who owns a business should be working towards an exit strategy. At first glance that might seem like a sweeping statement, especially if you have no current plans to sell or float your company.

But if we assume that at some point in the future you will want to cash in, then it makes sense to begin working early on the steps that will ensure that you achieve the best possible deal when the time comes to strike a deal. That means ensuring that your business presents the best possible face to the world. Some entrepreneurs begin preparations for exit from well before the first day's trading, but even if your forward planning doesn't quite extend that far, you should certainly use the years ahead of a sale to get the business in shape. What does that mean in practice?

You should be working to eradicate blemishes such as poor profit performance, bad debts, credit downgrades and any risk of being dragged through the courts by ex-employees. Going through the profit and loss account and balance sheet using ratios such as those covered in Chapter 12 will point out areas for improvement. You should try to make the three years prior to your exit look as good as possible. That means profit margins should be consistently high, the sales and profit curve should be heading upwards and strong financial control systems should be in evidence. There is nothing that puts buyers off quite as much as variable performance with profits oscillating all over the place. Even dramatic increases in profits or sales, way out of line with past performance, can cause problems. Buyers will suspect a one-off special situation and may decide to discount that in any estimate of value.

Once the business is firmly planted on a smooth upward trend, your future projections will look that much more plausible to a potential buyer. You should certainly have a business plan and strategic projections for at least five years. This will underpin the strength of your negotiations by demonstrating your skills and that of your management team in putting together the plan, and show that you believe the company has a healthy future.

There are a number of organisations that can help you to see how your business is likely to appear to a potential buyer. They include:

Ratios: Inter Company Comparison (www.icc.co.uk) and Jordans Limited (www.jordans.co.uk) provide regularly updated online company information services that enable users to access and retrieve data on individual companies, directors and shareholders. They also enable users to produce industry, group, peer and individual reports, allowing you to compare your business's performance with that of other similar companies as well as obtaining in-depth financial profiles.

Credit scores: Creditgate.com (www.creditgate.com) and Credit Reporting (www.creditreporting.co.uk/b2b) are among a growing number of companies that offer a comprehensive range of credit reports instantly online, including credit check, credit rating, company profile, credit score, credit reference, credit limit, company directors and CCJs (County Court Judgments). You can get your own business rating from one of these agencies to see how you look to the outside world.

Benchmarking: The Centre for Inter-firm Comparison (www. cifc.co.uk) helps businesses of every kind to improve their profitability and productivity by providing expertise in benchmarking, performance measurement and financial control. It gathers financial information on industries based on detailed information that has been provided – in absolute confidence – by participating firms on a comparable basis. That information is then provided showing industry average and best and worst performance standards, without of course revealing the individual participants' data.

CLEANING UP THE BOOKS

Private businesses do tend to run expenses through the business that might be frowned on under different ownership. One firm, for example, had its sale delayed for three years while the chairman's yacht was worked out of 'work in progress'. There can also be problems when personal assets are tucked away in the company, or where staff have been paid rather informally, free of tax. The liability rests with the company, and if the practice has continued for many years the financial picture can look quite messy.

To avoid horrors being uncovered in the due diligence process, you may need to 'clean' the company up beforehand. A change of auditors may be necessary if you have been using a sleepy, small local firm, especially if they have become particularly friendly. Entrepreneurs rarely see any value in the audit process. They view it as just part of the bureaucratic trappings of the state. The temptation here is to cut costs and have the cheapest auditing firm that can be found. In preparing for a sale, however, you would be wise to select a more inquisitive and thorough firm, with a reputation that is likely to be known and respected by potential buyers.

The basic purpose of an annual audit of financial statements is to make sure that a business has followed the accounting methods and disclosure requirements as laid down by the financial regulators. The auditor confirms that in a short report, stating that in their opinion the accounts provide a true and fair view of the company's affairs. The audit does not give a potential buyer a cast-iron guarantee that all is as reported and they will still want to do their own due diligence, but audited accounts provided by a well-respected audit firm will carry weight with a prospective buyer and their advisers, and without them a blue-chip buyer may not even consider an acquisition at all.

The Big Four international accountancy firms – Deloitte & Touche, Ernst & Young, KPMG and PricewaterhouseCoopers – are household names in the business world. The next ten, all substantial firms too, are Baker Tilly, BDO Stoy Hayward, Bentley Jennison, Grant Thornton, Mazars, Moore Stephens, PKF, Smith & Williamson, The Tenon Group and Vantis. These firms bob up and down and on occasions even dip out of the top spots in this list. *Accountancy Age* (www.accountancyage. com) compiles an in-depth survey to find the top 50 accountancy firms each year.

PRODUCING THE SALES MEMORANDUM

The sales memorandum is the initial marketing document, whose main purpose is to bring a purchaser to the negotiation table. It is in effect the window that you have been taking all the above steps to dress! The initial draft is written by the management and then polished up by your corporate adviser. It should:

- Make the business sound attractive and feature product literature, photographs, charts and tables.
- Be a source of solid information, but not overfull of numbers and analysis. The buyer and their advisers will get your accounts themselves.
- Show that the business has scope for improvement and development if someone with more money and wider skills and experience takes it forward. Otherwise it will be hard for a buyer to see what value they can add.
- Contain no detailed confidential information or commercially sensitive information, such as the name of customers or suppliers. No buyer will make a final decision on the basis of a sales memorandum, so the detail can be provided later to serious buyers only.
- Be tailored to meet the needs of different potential buyers. For example, competitors will know a lot about the industry and your products, so those don't need to be explained to them.

Cavendish, a corporate finance firm that has successfully completed some 400 company sales across a broad range of industry sectors and should know a thing or two about this topic, has a detailed brief for writing a sales memorandum as well as a table of contents on its website (www.cavendish.com), as well as a mass of other valuable pointers.

Goldsmith's – Working towards a sale

Mark Goldsmith and Simon Hersch started their catering wholesaling business from their halls of residence while they were still students at Manchester University. Taking advantage of a catering strike, they began supplying the student union with portioned cakes sourced from Robert's Fridge Factory, a small London-based manufacturer known to them. Buoyed on by their initial success, they produced a single-sheet leaflet entitled 'Earning More Bread is a Piece of Cake', with a smart Goldsmith's logo, and itemising on the reverse side the various small food items they could provide. This was distributed to small snack outlets in the vicinity of the university and became their primary marketing tool and calling card. Goldsmith's was built up carefully over the next decade, with the accounts being professionally audited. Goldsmith's (Northern) Ltd continued to provide Simon and his 40 employees with an interesting and rewarding lifestyle until its sale to Spring Fine Foods (www.springfinefoods.com).

GETTING THE TIMING RIGHT

As the last few years have demonstrated, timing is crucial when selling a business. Until the crisis in the US subprime mortgage market sparked first a credit crunch, then a full-blown economic downturn, business owners could be confident in the knowledge that they were enjoying a seller's market. With cheap credit easily available, trade buyers, corporates and private equity companies were on the look-out for deals and demand for businesses was high. Consequently, valuations soared. However, the credit crunch changed all that. Valuations tumbled again and it was not a good time to take your business to the market.

There is little point in getting into your t-shirt and shorts in the middle of winter. A recession is the economic equivalent of winter and it is pointless hoping for great value during one. The only people in the market are 'bottom dippers', those few cash-rich players able and willing to take the long view. Recessions mean belt tightening and job losses, but for the entrepreneur aiming to sell up, it's the state of the stock market that gives the best indication of when you can expect the best value. Since 1900 we have had 27 bull markets in company shares with corresponding bear markets. These ups and downs result in very steep curves, with business values oscillating by as much as 80 per cent with changes in the market's perception of value. Such movements can result in a halving of general P/E ratios and as that is a key element of the value equation, the price you could expect to achieve is likely to follow suit.

As these differences in value often have very little to do with the actual profitability of businesses themselves, just trying to grow the business is unlikely to be the only or even the best strategy for maximising the value of your business. While businesses listed on the stock market may not like these swings in value, they have no difficulty in working out what their businesses are worth at any moment in time – the value is published daily in the financial press and every few minutes on financial websites. But as most businesses, yours in all probability included, are not listed on a stock market, you can't easily keep tabs on market sentiment for the value of your business in that way. However, you can monitor trends on the BDO Stoy Hayward Private Company Index (www.bdo.co.uk).

Nevertheless, as the story of Thomas Goode shows, it is not always possible to pick the ideal time to sell up. Other and more pressing factors may come into play.

Thomas Goode – how the market affects the chances of a sale

Thomas Goode's business started in 1827, when the eponymous owner opened a china store in Hanover Square. The shop moved in 1845 to a site in South Audley Street and consisted of an enticing maze of small showrooms displaying ornate glassware, porcelain and fine china. Mrs Robinson, a former executive editor of *Vogue* magazine who also worked as a main board director at Debenhams, gradually transformed the business after her appointment as managing director and also brought in outside professional managers. They modernised the shop, speeded up service, introduced computer technology, achieved faster stock turnround and improved the availability of goods. They also introduced a range of branded goods, ranging from pottery to playing cards, and were looking at further licensing and franchising opportunities. Thomas Goode retained three royal warrants, which were proudly on display near the entrance. Other precious objects were also on show and two seven foot high Minton china elephants stood guard in the window.

However, the company reached an impasse, finding it hard to expand without further injections of cash. The company was hit badly by the collapse of a pottery manufacturer it ran in Stoke-on-Trent and an unfortunate – and expensive – attempt to stage an exhibition in the US on a day when Wall Street dived.

Like many other UK retailers, Thomas Goode suffered from the harsh trading climate in a recession and was further hampered when some large orders from Kuwait and Iraq were cancelled because of tensions in the Middle East. Sales in the company's final independent trading year rose from £3.4 million to £3.6 million, but the company still made a small loss at the pre-tax level.

After 164 years in business, Thomas Goode's 60 family shareholders decided that the business could best be taken forward as part of a larger organisation. They also wanted to realise some of the capital tied up in the business, which they hoped would fetch about £10 million. Hambros Bank was asked to look for suitable buyers and very quickly received several preliminary offers from potential purchasers in the UK as well as from North America, Japan and continental Europe.

WATCHING THE BUSINESS CYCLE

Sellers should watch the business cycle carefully. Put simply, economies tend to follow a cyclical pattern that moves from boom, when demand is strong, to slump, economists' shorthand for a downturn. The death of the cycle has often been heralded, as politicians believe that they have become better managers of demand, but the 'this time it's different' school of thinking has been proved wrong time and time again, most spectacularly in the autumn of 2008.

The cycle itself is caused by the collective behaviour of billions of people – the unfathomable 'animal spirits' of businesses and households. Maynard Keynes, the British economist whose strategy of encouraging governments to step up investment in bad times did much to alleviate the slump in the 1930s, explained animal spirits as: 'Most, probably all, of our decisions to do something positive, the full consequences of which will be drawn out over many days to come, can only be taken as the result of animal spirits – a spontaneous urge to action rather than inaction, and not as the outcome of a weighted average of quantitative benefits multiplied by quantitative probabilities.'

Added to the urge to act is the equally inevitable herd-like behaviour that leads to excessive optimism and pessimism. Typically, the optimism creates an economic bubble, which eventually bursts when pessimism sets in. From tulip mania in seventeenth-century Holland and the eighteenth-century South Sea bubble to the Internet bubble in 1999 and the collapse in US real estate in 2008, the story behind each bubble has been uncomfortably familiar. Strong market demand for some commodity (gold, copper, oil), currency, property or type of share leads the general public to believe that the trend cannot end. Overoptimism leads the public at large to overextend itself in acquiring the object of the mania, while lenders fall over each other to fan the flames. Finally, either the money runs out or

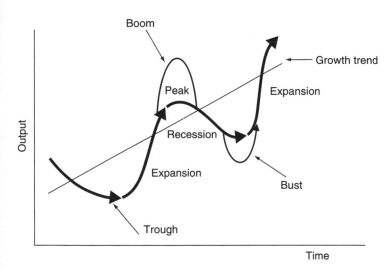

Figure 13.1 The classic economic cycle

groups of investors become cautious. Fear turns to panic selling, so creating a vicious downward spiral that can take years to recover from.

Economics is the science, in so far as it can be considered one, of the indistinctly knowable rather than the exactly predictable. Though all cycles, even the one you are in, are difficult to understand or predict with much accuracy, there are discernable patterns and some distinctive characteristics.

Figure 13.1 shows an elegant curve, which depicts the theoretical textbook cycle.

Difficult as it can be, you should try to take account of the business cycle when you formulate your sale plan. If you can sell at the peak, when valuations are high, that's great. Perhaps more importantly, avoid entering negotiations in a falling marlet.

Chapter 14

Pay day – selling up

It's the moment that you, and very possibly your backers, have been waiting for. You've knocked the business into shape and it's ready for sale. Now it's time to fire the starting gun and take it to the market.

Be prepared to spend time on this. There is a rule of thumb in the corporate finance business, covering the whole field of buying and selling businesses, that you will on average speak to 20 prospects before you conclude a deal. That's just the starting point. Once you narrow that field down to one or two potential buyers, there could well be some tough negotiating ahead.

The chances are that you will already know many of the people that you'll end up speaking to. Some will undoubtedly be competitors, but typically the sale of a business generates interest from trading partners up and down the value chain. Today's customer or supplier could be the company that buys your business tomorrow. You may also find that your employees are interested. Even in the current climate, private equity companies are keen backers of management and employee buy-outs, and news of a planned sale is often music to the ears of ambitious executives within the company in question.

Bear in mind, though, that while selling to people you know – whether an enthusiastic manager or an interested supplier – might be the easiest route to take, it won't always get you the best deal. You should look at all the options and take steps to generate interest in as many quarters as possible. But what exactly are those options?

TRADE SALE

Despite the apparent wide range of sales options, in practice the vast majority of companies are sold to other private companies – usually larger ones, and sometimes ones that are quoted on the stock exchange. These public businesses usually find that because they have better P/E multiples, it is cheaper to buy private companies than their fellow big fish. (See Chapter 15 where I cover floating on the market.)

Scientific instruments – selling to a larger group

From its origins in a garage, one small British manufacturer of scientific instruments managed to finance expansion from retained profits. Despite all the efforts of its management, however, the company faced three seemingly insuperable barriers to growth: it lacked the resources to develop its own computer systems; it was unduly dependent on one overseas supplier; and it was unable to break into the US market because its products were not sufficiently competitive. A new product that suffered from technical and design failings compounded these problems.

By the time the company was employing 20 people, it appeared to have reached a limit to its growth. It was helped out of this impasse when it was acquired by a larger company, so allowing the smaller firm to finance a new research and development programme and invest in production capacity. With the help of its larger parent, the smaller company has since grown to a turn-over of £11 million and a workforce of 245. Some 70 per cent of its production is exported and it is able to spend 12 per cent of turnover on R&D, thus keeping products at the cutting edge of its technology.

MANAGEMENT BUY-IN (MBI)

MBIs are where a capital provider, usually a venture capitalist (VC), backs an entrepreneur to buy into a company and effectively take it over. Usually the VC will have had a satisfactory relationship with the buy-in candidate in some other venture.

Amtrak – anatomy of a management buy-in

A former mail sorter who set up his own parcel delivery company with a £15,000 loan 11 years previously sold up for £86 million. Roger Baines, who left school at 15 to work for Hanson Parcels in Bristol, agreed to sell his Amtrak Holdings in a deal arranged by venture capital firm 3i. Baines built the company into what is now the UK's eighth-largest parcel delivery company, with a nationwide network of 330 franchises delivering 50,000 parcels a day. He has now retired to the Channel Island of Jersey.

Mick Jones, the ousted chief executive of Business Post, one of Amtrak's fiercest rivals, was brought in to run Amtrak as head of 3i's management buy-in team. Jones fell foul of a boardroom coup orchestrated by Business Post's Peter and Michael Kane after the brothers – who own 51.9 per cent of the company – returned from semi-retirement in Guernsey to take operational control of the company. They are now chief executive and managing director respectively. Jones said, 'I was sent home from Business Post on gardening leave in August and I have been sitting at home since, maybe playing the occasional round of golf. 3i had been scanning the newspapers, called me up and asked me if I would be interested. I immediately accepted – it's the perfect job.'

Jones was due to stay on Business Post's payroll for another nine months but has now severed all ties with the company and started work at Amtrak to help 3i achieve its plans to grow the business and float it on the stock market.

MANAGEMENT BUY-OUT (MBO)

This term is applied to the sale of a business to its existing management team. Buy-outs are where most venture capital providers put most of their money.

Upwards of 80 per cent of all venture capitalist investment goes into MBOs. It is not hard to see why they are so popular. The typical MBO is brought about by a large firm divesting peripheral activities to concentrate on its core business. The business being divested is usually well established and profitable, and the people in the best position to run the business are probably there already. Properly incentivised with shares and options, the existing team, now turbocharged, yield more profit than ever before. The result is much happiness and wealth all round.

Glass's Guide – moving forward through an MBO

The bible of Britain's second-hand car industry, *Glass's Guide*, was sold to an American investment company as part of a deal worth £126 million. The Glass's Group, which publishes the guide, was bought by Dallas-based Hicks, Muse, Tate & Furste. Almost every motor dealer in Britain carries a copy of the guide, which lists the value of thousands of different vehicles by age and model.

It was originally the brainchild of enthusiast William Glass, who begun noting down the value of sales at early car markets in the 1920s. Managing director Robin Oliphant explained, 'It was a time when the first cars were changing hands and there was no market or methodology to the pricing.'

The guide grew in popularity and Mr Glass established a business to publish it in 1933, which he ran until 1954. His family then managed the company for a few years until it was sold to the publishing giant Thomson. It changed hands again in 1995, when a management buy-out team led by Mr Oliphant acquired the business. Management continued to control between 20 per cent and 30 per cent of the company – a stake worth about £25 million to £35 million. The group provides software and databases that predict the value of cars in the future. It also helps businesses manage their vehicle fleets by forecasting costs for maintenance and accident repair. Mr Oliphant saw the takeover as the means to provide extra funds for expansion into Europe: 'We've always had ideas which have exceeded our shareholders' ability to fund them.'

Very small firms can often find it difficult to attract much venture capital interest in funding a buy-out. The reason is usually that the venture capitalist believes that the owner/manager makes all the key decisions, leaving the management to 'obey orders'. As the venture capitalist has no intention or desire to manage the business, it will be necessary to convince them that the existing management team can really run the business.

BIMBOS

This strange-sounding title stands for buy-in management buy-out. This occurs when some of a company's existing management team join with a new incoming managing director backed by a venture capital provider to buy the business. These are attractive deals for VCs as they get the best of several worlds. They get to put their own person in to run an established business, who is in turn supported by people who should know where the bodies are if anyone does.

You can find out more about BIMBOs, MBIs and MBOs from the Centre for Management Buy-out Research (CMBOR), founded by Barclays Private Equity Limited and Deloitte, at the Nottingham University Business School (www.nottingham. ac.uk).

FAMILY TAKEOVER

Less than 33 per cent of family businesses are passed on to the second generation and barely 13 per cent survive through to the third generation. So much for the bad news – the ones that do can be very successful. ALDI (short for Albrecht Discounts), Michelin, controlled and run by François Michelin, his son Edouard and their partner René Zingraff, and Mars, founded by

Minnesotans Frank and Ethel Mars who invented the Milky Way chocolate bar, are among the world's biggest family businesses.

If you have children or other family members involved in the business, they may well be the right people to take it over. Even if there is no obvious family succession candidate, it might be worth casting your net beyond the immediate family. One person attending the Cranfield Business Growth Programme wrote to all his family and relations, asking if anyone would like to join him. A stepdaughter accepted the challenge and quickly became a key member of the management team.

But you will need to plan how you will extract any value you want or need from that arrangement. It may be that you can allow them to pay for the company over a number of years, ideally before they take over all aspects of running the business.

You might be content to retain a shareholding and take your reward by way of a dividend. On balance a clean break is usually best, but in any event clear arrangements for payments agreed in writing is a prudent arrangement to ensure family peace. Succession planning in a family business can be difficult. One organisation that can help is the BDO Stoy Hayward Family Business Centre (www.bdo.uk.com).

Reed Personnel – keeping it in the family

Alec Reed, chairman of Reed Personnel, claimed that the recruitment industry hardly changed at all during his first 35 years in the business. Now change has come to both the industry and to his company, sparked initially by recession and hastened by new technology. Reed Personnel accelerated the change when Alec's son James was appointed as chief executive. The founder, who learnt his business and management acumen in the School of Life, passed on the baton to the Oxford and Harvard-trained new generation.

Alec Reed left Gillette 38 years ago, where he had risen from junior clerk to become divisional accountant. His former employers became his first client and had remained with the company ever since. Reed, like all successful entrepreneurs, was in the right place at the right time.

He opened his first branch in his home town of Hounslow and it went like a bomb. At first he didn't realise why, but his business was right in the middle of the battlefield for labour between traditional employers along the Great West Road and London's Heathrow airport, which had just opened and had a huge demand for staff.

Reed never assumed that any of his three children would join the business, but he recognised that there are undoubted advantages for everyone to keep the executive reins in the family. A key advantage is that a family business is focused on a long-term view rather than making a quick buck, and so creates stability for the staff and shareholders, while an employed chief executive may be in the company for less than a decade and has to make his name in a short space of time, perhaps to the detriment of the ultimate value of the company. Having handed over the daily running of the business, Alec Reed has more time to pursue his many interests, including the family charity, which is involved with a number of good causes. James Reed grew up aware of the family business, recruiting temporary and permanent staff. But a job with the family firm was by no means a foregone conclusion.

After graduating he worked at The Body Shop and Saatchi & Saatchi before joining the BBC as a trainee television producer. He might have continued a successful career on the small screen, but for his inheritance. 'I knew whatever I did I ultimately wanted to be in charge,' James Reed says. 'Reed had reached an interesting stage of development in a business that was changing very quickly. Like my father at Gillette I was feeling frustrated at the time, and he made the prospect of working in the firm seem very attractive.' It is difficult to separate family and working life when it is your own business. But James Reed sees it as a bonus: 'There's the motivation to make it as successful as you can because your name is above the door.'

EMPLOYEE BUY-OUT

There is a growing body of evidence that employee-owned businesses are more successful in terms of productivity and profits than most other forms of ownership. The logic is that the structure aligns the interest of owners and workers, creates an environment conducive to recruiting and retaining the best employees and makes long-term thinking possible, free of the pressures of short-run profit maximisation.

While all those outcomes may be true, an employee buy-out doesn't necessarily represent an exit strategy that maximises the wealth of the founders. As with all entrepreneurial wealth creation, it does at least give you a choice.

Loch Fyne Oysters – selling out to employees

Bruce Davidson's latest job is a far cry from the work he was used to, working in sales and marketing for global tobacco companies in the Far East. Joining Loch Fyne Oysters in 2006, Davidson's job was to push the company into new markets and develop the business without losing its founders' vision. The company was set up in 1978 by an unlikely couple, Johnny Noble who had worked at Warburg's, the merchant bank co-founded by his uncle, and Andrew Lane, a marine biologist living in a leaking caravan. Their start-up capital assets consisted of a small dinghy and a very secondhand wetsuit. By the time Noble died in 2002, aged just 65, the business not only comprised a substantial oyster bed farm in the clean waters of Loch Fyne warmed by the Gulf Stream, but ran a chain of 38 restaurants that had their origins in a roadside trestle table in a lay-by off the A83.

Both men, in their own way, were passionate about creating sustainable employment opportunities and championing rural Scottish produce. This dedication to the community continued when, following Lane's death, Noble was instrumental in ensuring that Loch Fyne Oysters was bought by its own employees. The restaurants were spun off and sold to the brewer Greene King for £68 million. There were plenty of buyers interested in buying the residue of the business, the oyster farms themselves and the oyster bar shop, with a turnover of £1 million a year run by Christine MacCallum, wife of the shepherd on Noble's estate. But the business with 130 employees was eventually sold off to its employees for £4 million in an employee buy-out masterminded by David Erdal, who had done the same for his own family paper mill and other medium-sized companies since, and underwritten by a fund created from the Greene King sale.

Davidson plans to increase turnover to somewhere approaching £50 million in the next five years, leveraging his experience in international markets. Far from finding the unusual ownership a handicap, Davidson

> sees employee ownership as being a help when times get tough as they won't have institutional investors breathing down their necks. The economic climate should provide plenty of opportunities to put that benefit to the test.

GETTING ADVICE

When doing anything for the first time it is always a good idea to get advice. There are plenty of corporate finance advisers around – many of them working for local and national accountancy firms – and all will have had experience buying and selling businesses. Depending on your requirements they can provide help with everything from preparing the business for sale, through to identifying potential buyers and the final negotiations. Indeed, if you're not a skilled negotiator, it may be wise to let the accountants or your legal team take the front seat.

Corporate finance expertise doesn't come cheap, though. Expect to pay out between 3 and 7 per cent of the value of your business, and to have to lay out a largish five-figure sum on the table to kick things off. Think of it as an investment. Good advice can easily double the amount of money you actually end up with when tax, pensions and warranties are taken into consideration.

There are a number of organisations that can help you find professional advisers and advice from those experienced in selling businesses:

- HW is a national business advisory and accountancy firm with a network of over 60 offices strategically placed throughout England, Wales and Scotland, offering advice on a range of financial matters including specific help with selling your business (www.hwca.com).

- Business Link (www.businesslink.gov.uk) has a comprehensive range of advice covering everything from preparing your business for the sale to handling potential redundancies, including links to sources of professional help.
- BDO Stoy Hayward, an accountancy firm, has a publication, *Guide to Selling Your Business* (available from www.bdo.uk. com), which sets out its service offer to entrepreneurs planning to sell up.

NEGOTIATING STRATEGIES

Selling a business can change your life immeasurably for the better, but if you feel in any way short changed it can leave you feeling dissatisfied. It's important to think carefully about exactly what you want or need from the sale and how you can best achieve the desired outcome through negotiation.

Negotiating the best price for your business or a stake in it follows much the same rules as with any other deal. The first thing to keep firmly in mind is to aim high from the outset. Raising a price once a buyer's expectations have been set at a lower level is virtually impossible. The investor will have gone up their chain of command to get approval in principle for the deal before they issue a term sheet and going back with a higher price will not exactly reflect greatly on them. Secondly, there are plenty of variables in any deal aside from the price: when and how the money will be paid, directors' employment contracts, profit warranties and asset valuations, to name only a handful.

You need to keep all of these in your mind and look for a mix that meets your requirements best. In addition, you need to keep looking for new variables to put into the equation. For example, if you find an investor is worried about the valuation because of uncertainty about your profit forecasts, you could introduce the idea of an earn-out, or raise the amount of any earn-out by introducing a ratchet, a scale that accelerates the value the closer you get to achieving your profit target. Finally, both parties need to be satisfied that have got a good deal. Word travels fast and far in the business world and no one likes to be screwed on a deal.

Agreeing on terms

The term sheet is the opening shot in negotiations and before you can go much further you need to reach broad agreement on:

- *Price:* The value of the business, the amount the investor will pay and the share of the business they acquire are central to the negotiation.
- *Control:* Investors will be looking for ways to control their investment, such as representation on the board of directors or some type of involvement in decision making. You as the entrepreneur have to decide how much control you can give up.
- *Performance measures:* You need to decide what measures and targets for success both you and the investors accept, and then you need to hammer these out (e.g. sales volumes, cash-flow levels, debt repayment).
- *Employment contracts:* Contracts to ensure that key players keep their positions may be part of the financing agreement.
- *Exit strategy:* You need to determine how and when the investor will be able to take their investment out of the business (e.g. sale of the company, initial public offering, share buyback).

Scrutinise legal and other obligations

Be sure to consider the following:

- *Legal issues:* Be sure you understand the legal implications of the agreement, such as what representations and warranties the company is prepared to give, the composition of the board of directors, the dividend policy, compensation arrangements and so on.
- *Government regulations:* Have your lawyer check that all applicable regulations, restrictions and registration requirements are considered.
- *Existing contracts:* See what effect the deal will have on existing contracts, such as licences, employment contracts, supplier contracts or bank loans.

PASSING THE DUE DILIGENCE PROCESS

Before closing the deal, the buyer or investor will conduct a due diligence review to verify your information and to obtain more data, if necessary. Every investor will perform the due diligence review differently. Some will have advisers (usually from large accounting firms) to perform the task, whereas others, often angels, will handle it themselves.

A due diligence review will usually include a detailed look at these main elements of your business:

- Financial review of your company's financial status.
- Management review of your management team's capabilities.
- Market review of your marketing plan and activities, customer status and order book.
- Operations and technical review of your equipment, plant, processes, pollution etc.

- Intellectual property review confirming ownership and value of key IP.

Your accounts have to be correct, tax paid up to date, mortgages declared and any lawsuits rumbling in the background for unfair dismissal of employees, disputes with suppliers or defective products supplied need to be flushed out into the open.

At the end of the due diligence process, lots of people end up with liabilities. The corporate finance firm and the lawyers are responsible for the quality of their advice; if they get it wrong they can be sued. The accountants are responsible on your side for delivering proper accounts and on the buyer's side for interpreting them correctly.

Sellers are usually required to give warranties and indemnities to the buyer to the effect that every important thing they have said about the business and its accounts is true, and that they have left nothing material unsaid. By way of guarantee, a portion of the selling price is not paid up for a period of a year or so, giving time for skeletons to be uncovered. AllBusiness (www. allbusiness.com) has resources for entrepreneurs, including a free 40-point due diligence checklist. You can buy the full Monty for $25. You should, of course, have done some due diligence of your own, to make sure the investor's reputation is sound.

What is an earn-out?

One trick that buyers and their canny advisers use to make sure that your business is really worth all the bundles of dough they are paying out is to make you do some of the hard work for them. The thinking behind this is that as you have been running the firm for years, no one is better qualified than you to make sure that you keep sweet customers and suppliers with whom you presumably have a good working relationship.

Typically, if an earn-out is proposed it is for between 10 and 30 per cent of the sale price and covers a period of between one and three years. The rule here is that sellers should resist such proposals and buyers should insist on them!

Most of the costs involved in selling your business are based on a percentage of the selling price. That figure includes the earn-out amount, whether or not the figure is actually achieved. There are also some unique tax implications that you or your adviser should check out with HM Revenue and Customs (www.hmrc.gov.uk).

CHECK OUT THE ALTERNATIVES

Trade sales and buy-outs are by no means the only ways to realise the value of a business. The success of London's Alternative Investment Market and its rival Plus Markets has meant that even relatively small companies have an opportunity to float their shares. That's what we'll be looking at in the next chapter.

Chapter 15

Floating off

By the time you have successfully grown your business to the point where profits are above £1 million, it will be possible to give some serious thought to floating on a stock market. That means selling shares in your business to the public at large and perhaps in time getting your company bought out by a bigger fish still.

There was a time when a stock market flotation was an option for only the very biggest companies. Today, however, London's Alternative Investment Market (AIM) is home to a great many companies that started small but are growing rapidly. If you need to raise capital and increase your profile, it is an option worth considering and one that is much less costly than the London Stock Exchange main list. Cheaper again is Plus, an independent stock exchange aimed largely at entrepreneurial companies.

WHY FLOAT?

Why would you favour a flotation, rather than a further invest-ment by private equity? The logic of the maths is as follows. Your business with a profit of £1 million would in all probability be valued at £4 million, give or take £500,000, based on a P/E ratio of 4. However, the same business on a stock market could be valued on a much higher P/E ratio, perhaps as much as double. The logic is that the shares are liquid; that is, investors know their value from day to day and can sell up and move on any time they like. Also companies on a stock market are subject to a greater degree of scrutiny and so investors can be more confident in their accounts. The market crash of October 2008 left that argument in some doubt, however.

You also have a powerful way to accelerate value once your company has been floated off. If you bought a private business that is making profits of £250,000 in your business sector, it would in all probability be sold on a P/E of around 4, so costing you about £1 million. But now that profit would be in a public company and as you are on a P/E of 8 it would add £2 million to your value ($8 \times 250,000$). In effect, for £1 million of invest-ment you have instantly added £2 million to your value; of course, the profit stream of £250,000 should continue and there may well be synergies from cost savings and economies of scale. That's the alchemy of market multiples.

GOING TO MARKET

Stock markets are places where serious businesses raise serious money. It is possible to raise anything from a few million to tens of billions; expect the costs and efforts in getting listed to match those stellar figures. The basic idea is that owners sell shares in their businesses that in effect bring in a whole raft of new 'owners' who in turn have a stake in the business's future profits. When they want out, they sell their shares on to other investors. The share price moves up and down to ensure that there are as many buyers as sellers at any one time.

Going public also puts a stamp of respectability on you and your company. It will enhance the status and credibility of your business, and it will enable you to borrow more against the 'security' provided by your new shareholders, should you so wish. Your shares will also offer an attractive way to retain and motivate key staff. If they are given, or rather are allowed to earn, share options at discounted prices, they too can participate in the capital gains you are making. With a public share listing you can now join in the takeover and asset-stripping game. When your share price is high and things are going well you can look out for weaker firms to gobble up – and all you have to do is to offer them more of your shares in return for theirs. You do not even have to find real money. But of course, this is a two-sided game and you also may become the target of a hostile bid.

There are other potential pitfalls. You may find that being in the public eye not only cramps your style but fills up your engagement diary too. Most CEOs of public companies find that they have to spend up to a quarter of their time 'in the City' explaining their strategies, in the months preceding and the first years following going public. It is not unusual for so much management time to have been devoted to answering accountants' and stockbrokers' questions that there is not enough time to run the day-to-day business, and profits drop as a direct consequence.

The City also creates its own pressure, both to seduce companies onto the market and then by expecting them to perform beyond any reasonable expectation. There have been a number of high-profile examples of companies that have floated their shares on a stock market then changed their minds and withdrawn, buying out all outside shareholders. The rationale for taking a company private is that the buyer feels that they can run the company better without the need to justify their decisions to other shareholders, or without the complex and burdensome regulations with which public companies must comply.

THE RULES OF THE GAME

The rules vary from market to market, but these are the conditions that are likely to apply to getting a company listed on an exchange.

Getting listed on a major stock exchange calls for a track record of making substantial profits with decent seven-figure sums being made in the year you plan to float, as this process is known. A listing also calls for a large proportion, usually at least 25 per cent, of the company's shares being put up for sale at the outset. In addition, you would be expected to have 100 shareholders now and be able to demonstrate that 100 more will come on board as a result of the listing.

As you draw up your flotation plan and timetable, you should have the following matters in mind:

- *Advisers:* You will need to be supported by a team that includes a sponsor, stockbroker, reporting accountant and solicitor. These should be respected firms, active in flotation work and familiar with your company's type of business. You and your company may be judged by the company you keep, so choose advisers of good repute and make sure that the personalities work effectively together. It is very unlikely that a small local firm of accountants, however satisfactory, will be up to this task.
- *Sponsor:* You will need to appoint a financial institution, usually a merchant banker, to fill this important role. If you

do not already have a merchant bank in mind, your accountant will offer guidance. The job of the sponsor is to coordinate the project and drive it forward.

- *Timetable:* It is essential to have a timetable for the final months during the run-up to a float – and to adhere to it. The company's directors and senior staff will be fully occupied in providing information and attending meetings. They will have to delegate and there must be sufficient back-up support to ensure that the business does not suffer.

- *Management team:* A potential investor will want to be satisfied that your company is well managed, at board level and below. It is important to ensure succession, perhaps by offering key directors and managers service agreements and share options. It is wise to draw on the experience of well-qualified non-executive directors.

- *Accounts:* The objective is to have a profit record that is rising, but in achieving this you will need to take into account directors' remuneration, pension contributions and the elimination of any expenditure that might be acceptable in a privately owned company but would not be in a public company, namely excessive perks such as yachts, luxury cars, lavish expense accounts and holiday homes. Bear in mind that accounts must be consolidated and audited to appropriate accounting standards and the audit reports must not contain any major qualifications. The auditors will need to be satisfied that there are proper stock records and a consistent basis of valuing stock during the years prior to flotation. Accounts for the last three years will need to be disclosed and the date of the last accounts must be within six months of the share issue. You need to be particularly careful with respect to stock valuations, as this is an area where mistakes are easily made and there is a temptation to tamper with the figures to reduce tax liability. The old accounts saying 'You tell me the profit you want and I'll tell you your stock level' is a dangerous trap, as the tax authorities are unlikely to check your stock physically unless they suspect fraud. Anyone endorsing your accounts for either a float or an acquisition is almost certain to dig much deeper.

FLOTATION OPTIONS

There are three main options when it comes to where to launch: a main market, a junior market or a small, specialist market that focuses on a specific sector or size of business. There are a number of key differences, the first and foremost of which is cost. Getting listed on the very smallest stock market will cost on average £150,000, a mid-sized market between £350,000 and £1 million, and a main market £1 million and upwards. The next difference is that main markets have greater liquidity and visibility than junior markets, which usually means that their shares trade on higher P/E multiples.

Main stock markets
These are the primary exchanges in the major financial centres and include the NYSE Euronext (the family of exchanges including the New York Stock Exchange, operating in six countries), Nasdaq (National Association of Securities Dealers Automated Quotations), the London Stock Exchange (LSE), the Tokyo Stock Exchange and the Deutsche Börse (DAX). The regulations are onerous for entering one of these markets and it is more usual to join a junior or specialist market first.

Junior markets
Pre-eminent in this sector is London's Alternative Investment Market (AIM), formed in the 1990s specifically to provide risk

capital for new rather than established ventures, and this is where many companies start out. AIM raised £15.7 billion last year – a 76 per cent leap from the previous year – and a record number of companies floated on the exchange, bringing the total to 1634. AIM is particularly attractive to a dynamic company of any size, age or business sector that has rapid growth in mind. The smallest firm on AIM entered at under £1 million capitalisation and the largest at over £500 million. The formalities are minimal, but the costs of entry are high and you must have a nominated adviser, such as a major accountancy firm, stockbroker or banker. The costs of floating on the junior market are around 6.5 per cent of all funds raised and companies valued at less than £2 million can expect to shell out a quarter of funds raised in costs alone. AIM is regulated by the London Stock Exchange.

More junior markets

One rung down from AIM is Plus, whose roots lie in the market formerly known as Ofex. It began life in 2004 and was granted Recognised Investment Exchange (RIE) status by the Financial Services Authority (FSA) in 2007. Aimed at smaller companies wanting to raise up to £10 million, Plus draws on a pool of capital primarily from private investors. The market is regulated, but requirements are not as stringent as those of AIM or the main market and the costs of flotation and ongoing costs are lower. Keycom used this market to raise £4.4 million in 2008 to buy out a competitor and gain a combined contract to provide broadband access to 40,000 student rooms in UK universities.

World stock market guides

You can check out all the world's stock markets from Australia to Zagreb on Stock Exchanges World Wide Links (www.tdd.lt/slnews/Stock_Exchanges/Stock.Exchanges. htm), maintained by Aldas Kirvaitis of Lithuania, and at World Wide-Tax.com (www.worldwide-tax.com). Once on the stock exchange's website, almost all of which have pages in English, look out for a term such as 'Listing Center', 'Listing' or 'Rules'. There you will find the latest criteria for floating a company on that particular exchange.

On the London Stock Exchange website (www.londonstockexchange.com), you will find all the information you need on the latest rules and how to go about finding a sponsor and adviser.

TIMETABLE TO A FLOAT

An Initial Public Offering (IPO), as the first launch of shares to the public is known, used to take about six months to execute, but now it is routinely being done in half that time. Though it may vary from exchange to exchange, the timetable looks broadly like the following.

Week 1
Pick underwriters to take your company to market. This involves listening to a dozen or more bankers tell you why they are No.

1 in doing your type of IPO. At the rate of three a day this can be a wearying experience, listening to depressingly similar presentations. The bankers will all have done successful IPOs before, probably by the dozen, so you will be looking more for empathy than technical competence. At the end of the week you need to have chosen a lead and probably a couple of co-managers to help spread the good word about your great business to the share-buying community.

Week 2

The lead manager begins drafting the company's prospectus. This involves sucking you, your management team and your accountants dry of background information. Your CFO will be involved full time in this process, so better get some financial back-up in place to deal with routine matters.

Week 3

You and your bankers collaborate on the prospectus. By now fairly junior staff will be handling the process. The stars you met on week one's presentations have moved on to sell the next deal. This process can involve several eight-hour days with people from your law, banking and accounting firms going through the documentation line by line.

This involves a delicate balance between outlining the risks and simultaneously describing the business and the investment prospects in a way that will appeal. You can see how other companies have gone about this process by looking at their filings on the London Stock Exchange and Securities and Exchange Commission (SEC) websites. In the end, the due diligence process should have flushed out any worries and concerns about you or your business.

Week 4

The lead manager files the registration document with the LSE/SEC, or its equivalent in whatever country you plan to list.

Weeks 5–8

The lead manager, bankers and you and your team prepare the roadshow presentation and wait for the LSE/SEC to digest your documents.

Week 9

The LSE/SEC responds with 20 pages of nitpicking questions, such as 'What do you mean by online response times?' and 'Can you provide evidence that your client X is one of the largest drinks manufacturers in Spain?' There may well be a second round of questions a few weeks later, but by now you will have got the measure of how to reply.

Probity is important in this whole process. What is required is transparency, the Nirvana of the share-dealing community. World Online's float on the Amsterdam Exchanges (AEX) in 2000 is a salutary warning on disclosure. The company was at the time Europe's largest Internet service provider. It generated an enormous amount of interest among Dutch private investors, the company's home base, with 150,000 subscribing to the March IPO at a price of €43. Within six weeks the price was down to €14.80. The reason given for the slump in price was that World Online's chairman, Nina Brink, had disposed of some of her shares to US private equity fund Baystar Capital three months before the float. The price she sold at was €6.04 and Baystar sold in the first few days of trading at over €30. Brink was accused of making allegedly misleading statements during the offer period and was forced to resign. Unhappy shareholders immediately reached for their lawyers.

Week 10

The lead manager plans the roadshow. You go to the bank and sell the company to its institutional salesforce. They then get to work with their clients to persuade them to subscribe for your stock. Everyone is bound by what are known as 'the rules' that govern the 'quiet period', which extends from due diligence until a set time after the IPO. Over this period the company must be careful about not hyping the stock or doing anything that would lead to speculation about your firm's performance in the press.

There are also rules explaining exactly what you can and cannot say to the press. It's generally best to say nothing. If one of your competitors is doing an IPO, its quiet period is a good time to hit at that company in the press, or to go out and buy a business that you know it might want. It is in effect in limbo and can't retaliate.

This is where the institutional sales team come into their own. Via an ancient ritual of winks, nudges, passive verbs, rhetorical questions and comparisons, they get their story across. The lead banks sales team can be a mighty force indeed. Goldman Sachs, for example, has several hundred front-line sales people in its IPO team, and that can result in a very big message reaching a lot of potential investors.

Weeks 11–12

A glorified travel agent in the bank fixes up a punishing schedule, known as the roadshow. This is the reverse of week 1, when people were selling to you. Now you are selling the stock to institutional investors. This could involve as many as 80 meetings across three continents in 13 days. A lot can be said at roadshow meetings, but the only document that can be handed out is the approved prospectus. Anything else could be a violation of the rules.

Commitments start to come in from the institutions: 'I'll take 250,000, but only if it's priced below £20. At £25 I'll only take 100,000.' The bank's syndicate manager has to make sense of this anticipated demand to come up with an IPO price.

Week 13

The day of the IPO. Assuming stock markets have not gone into one of their habitual nose dives, the bank's market maker figures out the highest price someone will sell and someone will buy at and sets a price, usually above the opening price and the price at which the institutions have bought at. If the markets have plunged and you have to pull the IPO, it's like slipping down a long snake back to the bottom of the snakes and ladders board. You may get another crack at it in six months, or perhaps never. One entrepreneur likened doing his IPO to childbirth: painful, glorious, but not to be done again.

Congratulations! Your company is now public, the bank collects 7 per cent of the proceeds, your employees are rich and you now have the funds and credibility to get back to growing the business and plan your final, gradual exit, unloading shares as you go.

However, if the market maker has got the price too high, and the shares plunge quickly, it will leave a sour taste in everyone's mouth. The pre-float shareholders can't realize their gain for months after the float, and having a paper profit slashed in half, as happened with Lastminute.com's float, will not endear you to the staff.

The institutions will be sitting on a loss, and while they are grown-up enough to take it on the chin, they will be very wary when you come back for more money. It is usually best to set the price at a rate that will see the shares rising in the weeks and months following a float. That makes for better press coverage too, which inevitably has a favourable impact on customers, suppliers and potential employees.

NCC Group – the road to a flotation

Not everyone was enthralled by either the economic downturn or the publicity highlighting the UK government's data protection failures. But to the NCC Group, which provides escrow software solutions, ensuring that business-critical material or source code is protected and accessible should anything happen to a key supplier, these factors helped grow turnover and 2008 profit to £35.7 million and £8.7 million respectively. The rise in turnover was helped by two acquisitions, but around a fifth of revenue growth was organic.

Rob Cotton, a chartered accountant with Coopers (now part of PriceWaterhouseCoopers) who is CEO, was headhunted by the National Computer Centre in 2000 to help the company develop its strategy for rapid growth. It didn't take Cotton long to see that the jewel in NCC's crown was the escrow business: this division, one of three, accounted for £8 million out of total sales of £12 million. By 2002 the company was due for another round of financing. The original venture capitalist (ECI), which had put in £3 million in 1999, had always envisaged a trade sale, but in 2002 the aftershock of the dot-com bust was still reverberating round the high-tech market.

So a management buy-out was decided on and five VCs were contacted and invited to fund the plan. By October 2002 Cotton had a shortlist of two, who came back at the end of January 2003 with their final bids. Those included banking details, investment levels, legal aspects and service agreements for directors. At the next round – after weighing up all the factors, the warranties, banking relationships and the people in the VC firm they would have to live with – it was decided to go with Barclays Private Equity. While the exact shape of the £31 million deal still had to be thrashed out, BPE was given a one-month exclusive period and their number two string was kept warm.

NCC's management, which was going to take the money and leave, fell out with aspects of the deal and refused to talk to Cotton for three months. Intensive negotiations with managers, VCs and everyone else concerned had to take place and the business, in a highly competitive market, still had to be run. Cotton says that the key for him was having a great corporate financier. The NCC Group had for some time been using Stuart Moss, a partner in Rickitt Mitchell, a local Manchester firm. Moss knew Cotton, the firm's technology, business and the personalities of NCC's management team. The parties were pulled back together and a rigid timetable got the deal concluded and the management paid off by April. Good professional advice saved Cotton 20 per cent in fees and was critical in resolving conflicts.

The company was admitted to AIM in 2004 and the main London stock market three years later.

ACCOUNTING RULES

Any company planning a market flotation should be prepared to comply with a stringent accounting regime. When preparing financial statements for its own internal use, a company has considerable latitude as to formats or methods of calculating individual figures. This is not the case with the preparation of the financial statements contained in the annual accounts and circulated to shareholders and other interested external parties of companies quoted on a stock exchange. These published accounts have to conform with certain regulations. Though the names will be different in other countries – in the US read Sarbanes-Oxley for The Companies (Audit, Investigations and Community Enterprise) Act, Securities and Exchange Commission (SEC) for the Stock Exchange – the regulatory bodies and the reporting principles are similar in all developed economies.

In the UK specifically, the rules on public company accounts are in the hands of three bodies:

1. Company law is laid down by Parliament in various Companies Acts, notably 1985, 1989 and 2006 – the longest act ever passed by Parliament (www.nortonrose.com); and The Companies (Audit, Investigations and Community Enterprise) Act 2004.
2. Accounting standards prescribed by the Financial Reporting Council (FRC), which comprise a set of professional rules governing the detailed calculations and presentation of information in published financial statements.
3. Stock exchange regulations augmenting the above bodies with their own additional requirements.

Listed companies are required to produce an annual report, the contents of which include the following main items listed below:

1. Chairman's statement – a broad review of progress, changes in strategy and management and a guide to future prospects. This may be supplemented by a chief executive's review of each individual business's performance.
2. Operating and financial review – a detailed commentary on the financial results and influential factors.
3. List of directors – details of service, responsibilities and other directorships.
4. Directors' report – a formal report on specific required items, e.g. dividend declaration, principal activities, share capital and substantial shareholdings, political and charitable contributions, directors' shareholdings, employment policy, creditor payment policy, close company status and appointment of auditors.
5. Report of the remuneration committee – policy statement on how the total remuneration package of executive and non-executive directors is set.
6. Corporate governance – a statement of compliance, or otherwise, with the Code of Best Practice on board structure and directors' remuneration. The original report by Cadbury was later supplemented with reports by Greenbury and then Hampel and was finally published by the London Stock Exchange in 1998 after seven years of discussion.
7. Auditors' report – a statement of the auditors' responsibility and their report on whether or not the financial statements give a true and fair view of the state of affairs.
8. Financial statements – comprising consolidated profit and loss account, balance sheet, cash-flow statement, statement of total recognised gains and losses and parent company balance sheet only.
9. Notes to the financial statements – additional breakdown and analysis of figures appearing in the main financial statements.

10. Historic record of financial performance – a 10-year summary of the main financial figures and ratios reflecting profitability, dividends and shareholders' funds.
11. Notice of meeting – notice of the time and venue of the annual general meeting and the business to be conducted.

WHY FLOAT?

Flotation is often the catalyst that moves a business on to the next level. In addition to its function as a means to raise cash, the enhanced profile generated by a listing can make it easier to secure big deals and attract experienced executives. It's not just a matter of profile. If you're in the market for talent, share option schemes can be as valuable a magnet as salary and bonuses.

Bear in mind, though, that a flotation shouldn't be seen as an exit. Yes, you can realise the value of the shares, but City investors would be nervous of any situation where the management team was using a listing as a means to bail out.

Chapter 16

Getting a second life

The deal is signed, the ink is drying and the lawyers and accountants have long since gone home. You've sold your company, you're considerably richer and a new phase of life has started. What happens next? The first step could well be that round-the-world trip you've always promised yourself, but what then? Entrepreneurs are seldom happy sitting around doing nothing, even if they have the wealth to do just that. So what are your options for a second life?

LIVING WITH AN EARN-OUT

The first thing that has to be said is that in very many cases the founder doesn't simply say goodbye to the business.

For instance, if the business you are selling is relatively young (say it's operated for up to five years), historical profits are low, potential performance is promising and the owner-manager is the most important business asset, it is likely that some portion of the sale price will be geared to future results. The logic is impeccable. Sellers obviously want to get the best price for their company and will base that price to reflect a prediction of future profits. Buyers are more likely to take a conservative view and base their offer price on past performance. If the two parties can't bridge the price gap, a potential way forward is to structure a deal to include an earn-out, where part of the total consideration payment for a business is deferred until the potential that the seller believes is likely is actually achieved.

Rather more than half of all private company acquisitions now involve some such arrangement. So this means that anything from six months to four years after your business is in new ownership, you could be staying on in some capacity or other. In the typical earn-out the purchaser will pay 60–80 per cent of the asking price upfront, with the remaining 20–40 per cent paid subject to the company achieving performance targets agreed by both parties within a designated period.

Creating a deal structure that in effect allows the negotiators to agree to disagree is not without risks, some of which can be serious, even fatal. The principal areas of risk are the following:

- *Operating tensions:* Sellers will want to see that they can manage the business to achieve their goals, that they will have adequate working capital and that the business won't be plundered to meet the purchaser's cash needs. Having committed its own capital upfront at least to a certain extent, the purchaser will want to ensure that the business is being run in a manner that it is happy with too. The business will have two masters and the former owner will have to face the prospects of becoming an employee in his (or her) own business, with an inevitable loss of power. Unsurprisingly, there will be tension, disagreement and perhaps conflict.

- *Incompatible horizons:* The buyer may be prepared to trade short-term pain for long-term gain in order to have a successful venture. The seller, focused on the short term, will be looking to maximise company performance during the earn-out period to enlarge his earn-out payment. The most obvious way this will occur is in the use of cash generated by the acquired business. The buyer will want to put that to use in the business and any surplus transferred out to the parent company. The seller will want it ring-fenced in an escrow account to guarantee its earn-out payment.

- *Inappropriate targets:* While appealing, it would be wrong to assume that it is in the buyer's interests to set the earn-out threshold as high as possible, as unrealistic targets can destroy staff morale and adversely affect performance. Also, it must be agreed exactly how performance is to be measured within the terms of the earn-out agreement. The new owner has ample opportunity to reduce declared profits by the use of management or central charges. Basing earn-out payments on gross rather than net profit can simplify the process considerably, and avoid potential disputes over the way profits are calculated. You may also consider using other methods to determine performance, such as cash flow or even the generation of new business.

- *Tying in staff:* As well as setting achievable targets, both buyer and seller need to offer incentives to key members of staff. The buyer can do this through stock options or performance bonuses, while the seller should consider allocating a portion of the earn-out to reward high-performing staff. However, any such payment could be subject to both income tax and National Insurance Contributions

(NICs), which could both dilute the incentive and demotivate staff.

- *Tax timing:* Earn-outs involve complicated capital gains tax (CGT) or income tax considerations, depending on the structuring of the deal. The seller should take early tax advice before negotiating the sale/purchase contract to optimise the tax treatment of the consideration. This should form an important part of the professional advice paid for in helping with the sale. There are plenty of tools to limit tax, but all are complicated and involve a degree of uncertainty.

Earn-outs are seldom achieved. Buyers and sellers often have to renegotiate the earn-out portion of the transaction over the period of the earn-out agreement. This can create much ill will and distract all parties from getting on with making the joint businesses successful. However difficult it may seem, sellers and buyers are best served if they can find a middle ground before concluding the deal so that both have certainty from the outset.

Life after the Big Cheese Company – a second start

The Big Cheese Company (BCC), set up by Robert Singleton, started trading from a 1200 sq ft converted butcher's shop in Lanark with just three staff. Robert's father had been in the cheese industry too, but his venture had not been a great success, so he counselled against going into this type of business. Robert saw a niche producing ready-grated cheese for the retail and catering market. His initial sales target was 3 tonnes per week and that was sufficient to make his company the first in the UK to grate cheese on a commercial scale.

Turnover in the first year was £500,000, with supply to the growing pizza industry accounting for 80 per cent of sales. Three years after its start-up, BCC moved to its second site on Cross Road, on the edge of town and close to the airport. This provided 25,000 sq ft of production, warehousing and office space, around twice the space Robert thought he would need for years ahead. The property was on the market as a result of the failure of another food business and it even had chill rooms, a cold store and some useful equipment thrown in with the sale. Robert and his advisers put together a business plan and raised the money through a venture capital firm to fund their growth. However, he had to get a mortgage for the premises, as the receiver who was selling it needed an immediate commitment and the price was rock bottom.

Within ten years the company's turnover had grown to £15 million. Throughout its history BCC put considerable effort into securing favourable publicity and brand building. It picked up six major awards, including the region's coveted Business Excellence Award two years running, as well as being nominated Best Business of the Year.

Robert (aged 42) reached the point where he felt he could no longer had the skills to maximise the business's potential, so he appointed BDO Stoy Hayward's corporate finance department to find him a buyer. He produced a short list of the dozen companies he felt could be interested, and in due course, after much negotiation, a small public company made an offer that valued his business at £10.5 million. BCC appealed to that company as it had just had an awful trading year. The chairman needed something positive to say in his year-end statement and BCC's £1.2 million profits would let him claim to be on track to maintain growth.

The deal included a two-year earn-out for £2 million of the £10.5 million sale price. Robert agreed, but was dismayed to discover on returning from a brief holiday to celebrate the sale that an interim managing director had been hired and was sitting in his office. He controlled the company's cash and had the managers reporting to him, and all that was left for Robert to do was to smooth the handover of key customer accounts to the new owners. The earn-out was based on profit and Robert had in effect lost control of the business, After three unhappy months trying to make the deal work, a pay-off of £500,000 was negotiated and Robert left. He has since set up a near identical business in another country and is well on the way to making his second fortune.

BECOMING AN ANGEL

Even allowing for an earn-out arrangement, the chances are that you will be looking forward to the future and wondering how you can occupy your time and your business brain. The answer for many entrepreneurs is to invest in other companies.

Having mastered the skills of entrepreneurship throughout the business cycle from innovation to wealth creation, sharing that knowledge and investing in the ideas of others can be satisfying and financially rewarding. Many entrepreneurs choose to do this through 'angel' investment.

Research has unravelled these sketchy facts about business angels as a breed. Knowing them may help you to decide if it's the right vocation for you:

- Business angels are generally self-made, high-net-worth individuals, with entrepreneurial backgrounds. Most are in the

45 to 65 age group; 20 per cent are millionaires; and only 2 per cent are women.

- On average they put less than 5 per cent of their wealth into such investments. For example, Robert Wright (see Chapter 11) invested less than £1 million after he sold up for £75 million. He invested in six businesses, two in the high-tech field and one being run by a couple of alumni from Cranfield where he studied for his MBA.
- 50 per cent of angels conduct minimal or no research on the business in question, meet their entrepreneur an average of 5.4 times before investing (compared with venture capitalists who meet on average 9.5 times), and 54 per cent neglected to take up independent personal references, compared to only 6 per cent of venture capitalists. Angels fundamentally back people and as it is their own money they can take as much risk as they have the appetite for. One angel, for example, has a pot of cash set aside for propositions that only need up to £5000. He makes decisions on these investments on the basis of just one phone conversation with the entrepreneur. He has a standard, simple contract and once this is signed he releases the cash. His argument is that if the business is successful it will need serious money and as his contract requires it to come to him first, he can do his due diligence then. If it fails, then at least he has saved wasting any of his time.
- Typically business angels invest 15 per cent of their investment portfolio in start-up business ventures and their motivation is, first and foremost, financial gain through capital appreciation, with the fun and enjoyment of being involved with an entrepreneurial business an important secondary motive. Only a minority are motivated in part by altruistic considerations, such as helping the next generation of entrepreneurs to get started and supporting their country or state.

GETTING A SECOND LIFE

- Business angels invest in only a very small proportion of the investments they see: typically at least seven out of eight opportunities are rejected. More than 90 per cent of investment opportunities are rejected at the initial screening stage.
- Around 30 per cent of investments by business angels are in technology-based businesses. Most will tell you that they vigorously avoid investing in industries they know nothing about.
- The majority of business angels invest in businesses located close to where they live and two thirds of investments are made in businesses located within 100 miles of their home or office. They are, however, prepared to look further afield if they have specific sector-related investment preferences or if they are technology investors.
- 92 per cent of angels had worked in a small firm compared, for example, with only 52 per cent of venture capitalists who had similar experience.
- On average, business angels sell their shareholding in the most successful investments after four years (and 75 per cent after seven years). Conversely, half of the investments in which business angels lost money had failed within two years of the investment being made.
- Business angels are up to five times more likely to invest in start-ups and early-stage investments than venture capital providers in general.

STARTING OVER – THE PATH OF THE SERIAL ENTREPRENEUR

Entrepreneurs under the age of 50 are very likely to explore the possibility of starting up in business again. After all, they have everything – energy, experience, contacts – plus something they didn't have when they started out before in the form of cash. And that cash can't be scaled up. You'd be astounded at how many more people want to put money into your venture once you have a successful track record.

VOLUNTEERING YOUR SKILLS

You don't have to put money making at the top of your priority list once you have sold up. Becoming a business angel investor or starting up another business are fine for those who still have an appetite for risk taking and a need for financial rewards. There are, however, all sorts of other rewards and bodies that recognise the value of entrepreneurial skills. For example:

- *Small business advisory organisations:* Enterprise Agencies in the UK and the SBA (Small Business Administration) in the US are among the many government or quasi-government organisations that are always on the look-out for mentors, tutors and advisers to local small businesses.
- *Charities:* Any charity would welcome the contribution that a successful entrepreneur could make. The Prince's Trust, an organisation founded by the Prince of Wales that helps younger and disadvantaged business starters to get going, is one of a burgeoning group of charities that focus on helping other entrepreneurs, as is the Blind Business Association Charitable Trust (BBACT). Or you could start your own charity. Entrepreneurs Unite, initiated by Virgin Unite, the independent charitable arm of Richard Branson and the Virgin Group, is an organisation that brings together like-minded entrepreneurs to invest in emerging markets and generate significant and sustainable social change. Profit is definitely not top of the list here. Microsoft co-founder Paul Allen has a foundation to help those with innovative ideas to

get started and the James Dyson Foundation will assist educational institutions working in the field of design, technology and engineering. Entrepreneur and *Dragons' Den* judge Peter Jones donated £100,000 to 'Make Your Mark With a Tenner', a government-backed campaign that aims to give young people the opportunity to become entrepreneurs.

- *Teaching in business schools:* Andy Phillipps, co-founder and CEO of Active Hotels, is entrepreneur in residence at INSEAD business school. He grew Active Hotels from its foundation in 1999 to become the largest online hotel-booking company in Europe. He sold the business to Priceline.com for $161 million in 2004 and was retained by to run the latter's international operations. He has subsequently helped establish, expand and/or invest in a number of start-ups, including Reevoo.com, I2O, Toptable and Moyses Stevens.

- *Advising governments:* Ministers are always on the look-out for successful entrepreneurs to chair or work on committees on business-related matters. Karan Billimoria, the founder of Cobra Beer, found time to chair and inspire a committee to advise the UK government on how to make Job Centres more focused on the needs of small businesses. He received a CBE and a year later became the first Parsi to take a seat in the House of Lords.

In other words, you have a whole lot of options to consider. You might want to take your time, parking your new-found wealth while considering what is right for you. The main thing is, enjoy yourself and take full advantage of your new life.

References

Herzberg, Frederick (1968) 'One more time: How do you motivate employees?' *Harvard Business Review*, January/February: 53–62.

Keynes, Maynard (2009) *The General Theory of Employment, Interest and Money*, BN Publishing. First published in 1936 in the UK by Palgrave Macmillan.

Levitt, Theodore (1960) 'Marketing myopia', *Harvard Business Review*, July/August: 45–56.

Maslow, Abraham (1943) 'A theory of human motivation', *Psychological Review*, 50: 370–396.

McGregor, Douglas (1960) *The Human Side of Enterprise*, McGraw Hill Higher Education.

Porter, Michael E. (1980) *Competitive Strategy: Techniques for Analyzing Industries and Competitors*, Free Press.

Schumpeter, Joseph (1962) *Capitalism, Socialism, and Democracy*, Harper Perennial. First published in 1942 by Harper and Brothers, New York.

Schumpeter, Joseph (1983) *The Theory of Economic Development: An Inquiry into Profits, Capital, Credit, Interest and the Business Cycle*, trans. Redvers Opie, Transaction Publishers,. First published in German in 1911 by Duncker and Humblot Leipzig.

Smith, Adam (2008) *An Inquiry into the Nature and Causes of the Wealth of Nations*, Forgotten Books. First published in the UK 1776 by W. Strahan and T. Cadell.

Tellis, Gerard & Golder, Peter N. (2001) *Will and Vision: How Latecomers Grow to Dominate Markets*, McGraw-Hill.

Resource list

Accountancy Age, www.accountancyage.com
Acquisitions Monthly, www.aqm-e.com
AllBusiness, www.allbusiness.com
All Conferences.com, www.allconferences.com
American Customer Satisfaction Index, www.acsi.org
Andrews University, www.andrews.edu
Applegate, www.applegate.co.uk
Ashridge Management College, www.ashridge.org.uk
Asset Based Finance Association, www.thefda.org.uk
Auditnet, www.auditnet.org
Australian Government, www.austradeict.gov.au
Bain, www.bain.com
BDO Stoy Hayward, www.bdo.uk.com
Belbin Team Roles, www.belbin.com
biz/ed, www.bized.co.uk
BizPep, www.bizpeponline.com

BizPlanIt, www.bizplanit.com
BizStats, www.bizstats.com
Boden, www.boden.co.uk
Bplans.com, www.bplans.com
British Business Angels Association, www.bbaa.org.uk
British Psychological Society, www.bps.org.uk
British Venture Capital Association, www.bvca.co.uk
Business.com, www.business.com
Business Expenses Guide, www.bytstart.co.uk
Business Link, www.businesslink.gov.uk
Buying Groups, www.buyinggroups.co.uk
Cavendish, www.cavendish.com
Central Intelligence Agency (CIA) *World Factbook*, www.cia.gov
Centre for Inter-firm Comparison, www.cifc.co.uk
Centre for Management Buy-out Research, www.nottingham.
  ac.uk
Chambers of Commerce, www.chamberonline.co.uk
Chartered Institute of Personnel and Development, www.cipd.
  co.uk
Collective Purchasing, www.collectivepurchasing.co.uk
Companies House, www.companieshouse.gov.uk
Corporate Information, www.corporateinformation.com
Creditgate.com, www.creditgate.com
Credit Reporting, www.creditreporting.co.uk/b2b
Dallas Capital, www.dallascap.com
Daltons Business, www.daltonsbusiness.com
Doing Business, www.doingbusiness.org
Easy Searcher 2, www.easysearcher.com
Esources, www.esources.co.uk
e-Three, www.e-three.com
Euro Info Centres, www.euro-info.org.uk
European Business Angels Network, www.eban.org
European Venture Capital Association, www.evca.com
Finance and Leasing Association, www.fla.org

Find Articles, www.findarticles.com
Flowcrete, www.flowcrete.com
Free Online Surveys, http://free-online-surveys.co.uk
Globe of Blogs, www.globeofblogs.com
Google, http://blogsearch.google.com
Google News, www.google.com
Google Trends, www.google.co.uk/trends
Harvard Business School, http://www.hbs.edu
HM Revenue & Customs, www.hmrc.gov.uk
Hotel Chocolat, www.hotelchocolat.co.uk
Haines Watts, hwca.com
Independent Director Initiative, www.independentdirector.
   co.uk
Interactive Investor, www.iii.co.uk
Inter Company Comparison, www.icc.co.uk
Internet Direct, www.internetdirect.co.uk
Internet Public Library, www.ipl.org
Inventory Overture, http://inventory.overture.com/d/search-
   inventory/suggestion/
Jordans Limited, www.jordans.co.uk
Kelly's, www.kellysearch.co.uk
Key Note, www.keynote.co.uk
Kompass, www.kompass.com
Lexis-Nexis, www.lexis-nexis.com
Link2Exports, www.link2exports.co.uk
London Stock Exchange, www.londonstockexchange.com
Microsoft (demographics), http://adlab.microsoft.com
Mintel, www.mintel.com
National Statistics, www.statistics.gov.uk
National Venture Capital Association, www.nvca.org
Net MBA, www.netmba.com
Norton Rose, www.nortonrose.com
Oneworld Health, www.oneworldhealth.org
Online Newspapers, www.onlinenewspapers.com

Pinchot & Company, www.pinchot.com
Power Purchasing Group, www.ppg.co.uk
ProShare, www.proshareclubs.co.uk
Real Business, www.realbusiness.co.uk
Research and Markets, www.researchandmarkets.co.uk
@ResearchInfo.com, www.researchinfo.com
Responsibletravel.com, www.responsibletravel.com
Royal Bank of Canada, www.royalbank.com
School for Social Entrepreneurs, www.sse.org.uk
Schwab Foundation, www.schwabfound.org
Score, www.score.org>Business Tools>Template Gallery>Break
  Even Analysis
Solution Matrix, www.solutionmatrix.com
SoOrganic, www.soorganic.com
Spring Fine Foods, www.springfinefoods.com
Stock Exchanges World Wide Links, www.tdd.lt/slnews/Stock_
  Exchanges/Stock.Exchanges.htm
Strategic Planning Institute, www.pimsonline.com
SVM, www.strategyvectormodel.com
The Funded, www.thefunded.com
The Work Foundation, www.theworkfoundation.com
Thomas Global Register, www.thomasglobal.com
Trade Association Forum, www.taforum.org
Venture Investment Partners, www.ventureip.co.uk
World Challenge, www.world-challenge.co.uk
World Market Research Associations, www.mrweb.com
Worldwide Tax, www.worldwide-tax.com
Zoomerang, www.zoomerang.com

About the Author

Colin Barrow was until recently Head of Enterprise Group at Cranfield School of Management, where he taught entrepreneurship on the MBA and other programmes. He is also a visiting professor at business schools in the US, Asia, France and Austria. His books on entrepreneurship and small business have been translated into 20 languages, including Russian and Chinese. He worked with Microsoft to incorporate the business planning model used in his teaching programmes into the software Microsoft Business Planner. He is a regular contributor to newspapers, periodicals and academic journals such as the *Financial Times, The Guardian, Management Today* and the *International Small Business Journal*.

Thousands of students have passed through Colin's start-up and business growth programmes, going on to run successful and thriving enterprises and raising millions in new capital. He is on the board of several small businesses, is a university academic governor, and has served on the boards of public companies, venture capital funds and on government task forces.

Other titles by Colin Barrow:
Incubators: A Realist's Guide to the World's New Business Accelerators
Starting a Business For Dummies
Understanding Business Accounting For Dummies

PUBLISHER'S ACKNOWLEDGEMENTS

The publisher would like to thank Trevor Clawson for the development work carried out.

Sources for newspaper headlines quoted on back cover:

Bebo:
Telegraph.co.uk
19th March 2008
Bebo was sold for £417 million. The founders *'are understood to own a 70 per cent stake in Bebo, which would see them receive about £290 million from the deal.'*

Foxtons:
Guardian.co.uk
21st May 2007
'The founder of London's largest estate agency Foxtons today sold the business to a private equity firm in a deal believed to have netted him a windfall of around £370m.'

Bodyshop:
The Independent
17th March 2006
'Cosmetics retailer Body Shop today agreed to a £652.3 million takeover by L'Oreal.'

Index

margin 109
measures 39
Saga 119
Sainsbury 127, 131
salary 90, 169, 176–7, 191, 245
sales
  budget 158
  forecasts 78
  manager 126, 157
  memoranda 205–6
  projections 78
  reports 101
  revenues 137, 156
  volumes 225
Sarbanes-Oxley 243
scaleability 12
School for Social Entrepreneurs 28, 260
scrutinise 226
Securities and Exchange Commission 243
security 68, 88, 111, 115, 118, 231
selling businesses 213, 223
service agreements 242
share
  buyback 225
  capital 92, 96, 109–10, 244
  option schemes 245
  price 111, 192, 230–1
Small Business Administration 254
Smith, Adam 167
SocGen 184
Sony 45
staff 14, 18, 71–2, 120, 127, 169, 178, 182, 204, 220, 241, 248–9
start-ups 72, 100, 250, 253, 255
statistics 27, 61, 68, 148, 166, 170, 172

stock
  exchange 199, 214, 243
  level 233
  options 248
strategic alliance 82
Strategic Planning Institute 124, 260
strategy 2, 16, 18, 34, 41–2, 45–7, 51, 74, 81, 108, 132, 134–6, 138–9, 141–2, 152, 165–6
substitute products 138
  see also product
success rate 170–1
  see also failure
succession planning 219
Superbrand Council 45
suppliers 18, 48, 50, 57, 61, 69, 71, 75–6, 135, 145–8, 151, 159, 163, 206, 213–4, 227–8
surveys 11, 30, 54–6, 186

T
tax
  audits 102
  authorities 233
  liability 233
  regime 147
team
  members 174
  work 179
technology 9, 18, 22, 25, 50, 88, 100, 123, 133, 183, 215, 219, 255
term sheet 101–2, 224–5
Tesco 131
test marketing 137
Thomas Global Register 61
threat 48
Toyota 43
track record 74, 78–9, 232, 254

271